GENDER-BALANCED BELIEF

A NEW ETHIC FOR CHRISTIANITY

MAVIS ROSE

Published in Australia by
Coventry Press
33 Scoresby Road
Bayswater VIC 3153

ISBN 9780648982258

Copyright © The Estate of Mavis Rose 2021

All rights reserved. Other than for the purposes and subject to the conditions prescribed under the *Copyright Act*, no part of this publication may be reproduced, stored in a retrieval system, or transmitted in any form or by any means, electronic, mechanical, photocopying, recording or otherwise, without the prior permission of the publisher.

Catalogue-in-Publication entry is available from the National Library of Australia http://catologue.nla.gov.au

Cover design by Ian James – www.jgd.com.au
Text design by Coventry Press
Set in Tex Gyre Pagella (Palatino) 11.5pt

Printed in Australia

Contents

Preface	iii
Introduction	x
1. A New Millennium Dawns	1
2. Christianity's Credibility Crisis	21
3. Women Seeking Justice	45
4. The Devaluation of Christian Women	75
5. The Embodiment Problem	102
6. The Cost of Dissent	134
7. The Importance of Gender Balance in Belief Systems	160

Preface

Revd Dr Josephine Inkpin

It has been well said that history, rightly understood, can either reinforce the walls of our confinements in the present, or become the gateway to a more flourishing future. History is also partly what we ourselves help to create, supported or bound by the specific contexts in which we live. This is part of the significance of this book. For it was written by one who herself made history with others, enabling a significant reshaping of the hitherto mono-gender ministry of her Church. In this, the author helped open gates for others.

Yet the achievement of the ordination of women, in the greater part of the Anglican Church of Australia, was, for Mavis, but a staging post. It was a vital symbol and expression of hope and progress. It was, however, only a start. As Mavis outlines in the following pages, it is not enough to have a few female faces at the table, even when they might come to wear episcopal mitres. If the walls of the house, its language and protocols, remain the same, there is no real freedom. Rather we are called afresh to new ways of seeing, being and doing. For the much wider and deeper struggle was, and remains, what the Bible calls shalom: healing, justice and peace for all.

Renewing the vision

Sadly, I met Mavis only once, in her final years, but it was a highly significant occasion. For she came to my home on the St Francis Theological College campus in Brisbane to talk with younger women about the lessons and legacy of the past. Indeed, in particular, Mavis was seeking to pass on to others her rich archive of recordings and other materials related to the Movement for the Ordination of Women. This book is another expression of that fresh mothering of the spirit of loving affirmation and transforming equality that she sought to rekindle and nurture in others. It is much needed. For, as we quickly recognised in meeting and in subsequent reflections, the women's movement has encountered new obstacles in its development in recent years.

Part of this is the result of some women entering into official priestly, and episcopal, positions and being drawn away from the larger vision of *shalom* by the pressure of work and demands upon them to show themselves 'as good as the men'. Part of this comes from a loss of connection with the struggle that enabled such first steps. Even among women in formation for the priesthood, and some of those women more recently ordained, there is a lack of knowledge of what has gone before. Consequently, many are condemned to repeat the learnings of the past, and to attempt to reinvent the wheel.

Mavis recognised this. This book is, therefore, a contribution to renewing the wider deeper vision and re-empowering women of all kinds, and their other-gendered allies. It is an important complement to Mavis' work on the hard-fought-for evolution of women's ministry, as in her book *Freedom from sanctified sexism: women transforming the church* (MacGregor, Qld. Allira, 1996), placing those developments in the bigger context and the continuing work of change.

Continuing changes and intersectionality

Undoubtedly, a number of things have changed, for good and ill, since Mavis completed this book in 2010. Notably, in relation to the title itself, there has been a shaking of foundations in the very conception of gender itself. As a transgender female priest, I witness to this personally, as gender diverse people emerge from the shadows of their own experience and, in new ways, transform received binary and other fixed assumptions of gender. Whilst 'gender balance' is therefore still profoundly lacking in both religious and wider spheres, that very aim is also being reconfigured. Gender has become a multi-dimensional kaleidoscopic reality rather than a more two (or even three) dimensional conception. This does not all undermine Mavis' own renewing vision of equality, but it does give it further depth, variety and nuance. Crucial issues of naming, power and exclusion identified by Mavis are both widened and made more complex.

The upshot in recent times has been the rise of intersectional thinking about gender, as various human particularities have come to the fore. The lively strength of women's insight and conviction in this book has thus been added to by fresh voices – among them womanist, postcolonial, gender diverse, queer, dis/ableist, interfaith – which have further illuminated women's struggles and enriched feminist thought and action.

What Mavis' work does is to help make a bridge, particularly for progressive people of faith, between second wave Christian feminism and such contemporary developments. Focus has shifted from church structures, even the sacramental importance of ordination, onto these wider issues. Mavis offers us here a way of understanding of how and why we would make this journey. Whilst not explicitly addressing them all, she shows how women like her, and other gendered allies, continued to work on the larger and more complex project of human spiritual and social renewal.

New challenges

Ironically, and sometimes tragically, as different women's voices have begun to be more articulated and partly heard, there have also been tensions among those seeking a better gender balanced vision of humanity. 'Identity politics' and new culture-clashes have altered patterns of commitment and thrown up new battlelines. Within religious spaces in recent years, conflicts over sexuality and its control have thus taken over from female-specific issues at the centre of much debate and wrestling for power and liberation. The call to value a greater range of human differences has, therefore, been used by opponents of gender balance to create divisions between groups which are seen as their common enemy. This has helped neither the movement of progressive women of faith, nor their real, and potential, allies, weakening them both. Mavis' words thus do not incorporate all aspects of contemporary intersectional feminist struggle. They do, however, powerfully affirm the need for shared understanding and common action.

Indeed, another aspect of profound change from the date of Mavis' writing is the rise of populist and sectarian ideologies, in both political and religious forms. Despite reactionary pressures, when Mavis wrote in 2010, a positive view of possible changes within many national and international bodies was easier to hold. Ten years on, even without the 2020 challenges of the COVID-19 pandemic, multilateralism and optimism are harder to cultivate. Populist authoritarianism, suspicion of expertise and institutional change, resurgent patriarchal violence, and environmental crisis denial, are rampant in many places.

In this book, Mavis thus rightly affirms the value of bodies such as the World Council of Churches in supporting women and addressing key issues, notably through the Ecumenical Decade of Churches in Solidarity with Women (1988-1998) and the Decade to Overcome Violence: Churches Seeking Peace and Reconciliation (2001-2010). The last decade has, however, seen a retreat from such ecumenical endeavour, with the growth of resistance to global structures and networks generally, and fresh emphasis given by religious bodies to denominational survival and to inward-looking, and/or sectarian approaches towards wider society. In the age of Facebook, Twitter and Google's hegemony, and in the face of cyber-warfare, Mavis' confidence about the creative value of (the then) emerging social media and contemporary communications has also been turned on its head in many respects.

Valuing a legacy of love

It is important to remember the major changes and fresh pressures of our contemporary world in pondering what Mavis still has to say to us. Yet, whilst there are fresh, positive and negative, features, we cannot move forward, however, without reflecting on where we have come from and what that journey still has to say to us. This was part of the reasoning in the World Council of Churches' own revisiting, in 2018, of the Ecumenical Decade of Churches in Solidarity with Women.[1] Similarly, we all need to recall the historical journey of building a just community with gender balance in order to strengthen collaboration in reading the signs of our times and acting more effectively within them. This book is thus both a powerful legacy of love on which we build and a key to assist us in unlocking, and moving, into a brighter future.

Mavis wrote clearly and intelligently, just as she thought and acted. What she offers is, hence, a continued prophetic plea for the reconstruction of both faith and society. It is not a mere memoir of where she had travelled, but a call to enter into a renewing future. She states the questions and her approach with poise and much precision. She draws widely

---

[1] https://www.oikoumene.org/en/press-centre/events/20th-anniversary-of-ecumenical-decade-of-the-churches-in-solidarity-with-women

on sources across the ecumenical spectrum and beyond. Above all, she speaks to us, 'as outsider and insider', out of a highly engaged and engaging experience of struggle and openness to others. Ten years on, there have been some causes for celebration, as well as reminders of entrenched resistance and the consolidation of reactionary bodies such as GAFCON (the Global Anglican Future Conference) within the Anglican Communion.

At the time of writing, there are fresh Australian signs of life such as the Australian Collaborators in Feminist Theologies,[2] and new Anglican women's initiatives. These Mavis would warmly welcome and rejoice in. Like this book, they are batons and signs of hope to pass on to today's #metoo generation and those who will come after. A great English working-class feminist, Ada Chew, used to say that feminism, or what Mavis called 'gender balance', was 'a long row to hoe'. What matters is that we keep on tending the garden. This is an inspiration to understand what has been planted, further to prune and nurture, and to keep sowing seeds for the future.

> *The Revd Dr Josephine Inkpin is a Lecturer in Theology at St Francis (Anglican) Theological College Brisbane. She was a former staff member of the national Council of Churches in Australia and General Secretary of the NSW Ecumenical Council. She is a former active member of the Movement for the Ordination of Women in England and is married to one of the first female priests, the Revd Penny Jones.*

---

[2] https://divinity.edu.au/centres-networks/feminist-theologies

Introduction

In 2000, considerable discussion took place concerning the direction Christianity might take in the new millennium. It was evident that the religious vacuum left by the decline in mainstream Christianity was, to some extent, being filled by diverse religious groups, borrowing from nature religions, Asian belief systems and even from space fiction. While spirituality was still valued, traditional forms of Christianity were losing appeal, especially in the teenage to fifties cohort. The task facing mainstream Christian leaders was how to achieve relevancy in an environment where younger people were much less doctrinally inhibited than in the past. Church leaders hoped that the pendulum would swing back to mainstream Christianity because of its ancient heritage and the roots so deeply implanted globally over two millennia. But by the end of the first decade of the 21st century, the decline in mainstream Christianity continues, although in some areas, such as fundamentalist Pentecostal churches, there is still a strong following.

The information revolution – where people have access through internet to extensive knowledge about the past and present state of the universe – has undoubtedly affected how people view religion. There is a greater demand for church doctrine to be based on factors which are reasoned and empirically proven. Supernatural and ancient myths from biblical texts which sustain religious faiths are increasingly viewed with scepticism. Nevertheless, there does appear to be an acknowledgment among people trying to fathom the deeper aspects of their life, that there exists a spiritual dimension which transcends the limits of human understanding. It is this search for ultimate meaning which people seek the freedom to explore, if necessary through paths that lead them away from mainstream religion.

What is especially difficult for conservative Christian leaders to accept is that any reform processes undertaken will require a change of mind-set and culture at all levels of existing ecclesial structures. The reforms carried out cannot be of the 'bandaid' variety; they must intrude into strongly protected areas, such as ecclesiology, doctrine and biblical interpretation. Gender issues – usually regarded as more akin to the secular sphere than the religious – must be high on the list of reform processes. Women have long been the backbone of Christian churches, but have received scant recognition for their contribution. It is not surprising that it has been churchwomen who have been pressing hardest for change during the twentieth century, especially in the final three decades. Women have suffered most from sanctified biological mythology.

As it evolved, Christianity became an extraordinarily male-centred religion, although there is scriptural evidence that this was not how Jesus Christ originally intended his religious movement to develop. Jesus never exalted masculinity. He was an egalitarian leader, who encouraged all people – irrespective of sex, class or ethnic group – to be his followers, helping him to establish universally the domain of God. The verses in the New Testament which subordinate women were written many years after Jesus' death.

Women were prominent in founding many of the early church communities. As Christianity survived and became publicly acceptable, women leaders were pushed aside by men who wanted Christianity to fit the male-dominant structures that were the norm in secular society. Masculinity gained divine status as Christianity increasingly adapted to the patriarchal Roman imperial system. The still highly esteemed early Church Fathers theologised the devaluation of women, sinking to almost obscene vilification of the female body.

As increasing numbers of women undertake theological studies today, they are astounded that such unsubstantiated negative statements about women could have been maintained, even reinforced, over two millennia. The Reformation period may have changed the practices and doctrines of Christianity, but it did little to enhance the status of women. The reluctance of clergy today, especially in the two oldest denominations, Roman Catholicism and Eastern Orthodoxy, to allow women entry into positions of church authority, is largely due to inbred gender bias which was always theologically flawed. Jesus never instituted male hegemony.

My research into women in Christianity has convinced me that gender issues are playing a significant part in the decline of mainstream churches. The feminist movements of the late nineteenth and twentieth centuries were major and influential events. They alerted women to the detrimental effects of sexual discrimination. Feminism did not stop at the church gate; it was absorbed into the psyches of millions of churchwomen. Women who had laboured devotedly for the church began to query why their efforts received minimal recognition while churchmen were highly respected, whether they performed well or not. When churchwomen alerted church leaders to the gender injustices that existed in most Christian ecclesial systems, they were accused of the sin of secularism and self-promotion.

Once churchwomen became aware of discrimination, it was difficult for them to remain spiritually attuned to the old worship forms. The male dominant content of liturgies, hymns, sermons and Bible readings were a constant reminder to women of inbuilt bias. Women quietly slipped out of church pews in search of more soul refreshing pastures. When they left, their husbands and children tended to follow them. Church leaders had failed to take into account the reality that women traditionally have been more stringent about church attendance than their spouses.

There is still a noticeable reluctance on the part of church leaders to redress the gender imbalance that is so deeply embedded within most church structures. Christian leaders – because they are so inured to working in a milieu dominated by male bodies and male theological perspectives – are reluctant to accept that gender imbalance is a major contributing factor to church decline.

Today, women in developed societies are winning top places in universities and entering professions once reserved for men, including politics, law and medicine. For Christianity to embark on the road to recovery, attitudes towards churchwomen must change, not only because the status of women in society generally is improving but because it was always against the ethics of Jesus Christ that women be regarded as inferior human beings.

The dearth of younger women has led to a generational imbalance in parishes. Women have for centuries been the mainstay of Christianity, the people who carried out the housekeeping and catering chores, the secretarial duties, the fundraising and the religious education of children. When young mothers are missing, parishes lose momentum. Sunday school numbers decline, younger husbands drop out and there are insufficient people to take over from the elderly parish workers who make up the majority of present churchgoers.

Male clergy numbers are also declining, especially in denominations which require priests to be celibate. The injustice of gender discrimination in church structures is highlighted when churchwomen are invited to take on responsible pastoral duties due to a shortage of male clergy, yet are at the same time denied official recognition. Ordination to the level of deacon, a ministry for women which was sanctioned in the Early Church, is still denied to females in the major mainstream Christian church, Roman Catholicism.

Religious nonconformity is developing into a social norm in the twenty-first century. The growth of non-mainstream worshipping communities – some predominantly Christian, some more eclectic – is a widespread phenomenon as people seek freedom to communicate with the sacred in ways they find to be spiritually fulfilling. Many women continue to worship Jesus Christ because they can empathise with him, seeing him as a person who walked on the fringes of his religious establishment, stressing that love and justice were the highest ideals in the domain of God.

Much of what I am recording in this book is related to the struggle of Christians, women and men, to achieve regeneration through correcting the flaws in ecclesial systems. My work has at its core a belief that Christianity is redeemable and that Jesus Christ is a relevant and vibrant role model for the new millennium. This book is, to a certain extent, an extension of my previous work, *Freedom from Sanctified Sexism*, a history of women in the Australian Anglican Church from the end of the nineteenth century up to the end of 1992, when women were finally admitted to the Australian Anglican priesthood. During the period of my doctoral research, I was personally deeply involved in Anglican and Catholic women's ordination groups. I was also in dialogue with women of other Christian denominations, including the Eastern Orthodox churches.

From my research findings and personal experiences confronting church leaders who opposed the entry of women to ordained ministry, I grew to respect and sympathise with women who had left the Church because they could no longer worship in a religious milieu in which they were so blatantly undervalued.

In this work, I have tried to play down my Anglican background and write across the Christian denominational boundaries. It may be considered *religiously incorrect* for me to critique those sections of Christianity where I am not officially a member, but I make no apologies for this. One of the blessings that Christian women have discovered through their struggle for gender balance and church renewal is that they must act in solidarity with one another. Denominational barriers were part of church*men's* history and politics. The major splits in Christianity date back to periods when women had minimum input into church affairs and decision-making. Women of faith are today seeking God's justice in ecumenical solidarity. As women interact increasingly across denominational borders, progress in one denomination spurs on women's activism in other churches.

Certainly, in the 21st century, there is much greater opportunity to be open in religious discussion. Lay people are frequently dialoguing with each other within and without church walls. Freedom to communicate is a basic human right which has not always been encouraged in religious circles, such as the Papal ban on discourse regarding priestly celibacy and the ordination of Catholic women. Communication networks, such as the Internet, allow such bans to be ignored. The old centralist pattern of church information being disseminated from the top down is under challenge from cyberspace.

Unfortunately, access to cyber space is not always available to people in technologically disadvantaged countries. A most worrying phenomenon of the Third Millennium is the huge disparity which exists between the rich and the poor, to a large extent due to past colonial exploitation. Interestingly, Christianity today is most vibrant in less developed countries, particularly on the African continent and in South America, perhaps because the poor gain hope from Jesus' message of love and outreach to those in need.

Churches have performed well in the area of practical relief to the disadvantaged peoples of the world. However, to achieve gender balance in underdeveloped nations, the focus needs to be on liberating women from structured powerlessness, violent abuse and illiteracy. Christian men are still reluctant to prioritise the special need of economic empowerment of Third World women if they are to break the long cycle of poverty and debasement they have suffered and in particular to prevent the practice of sexual enslavement.

Religious leaders of all denominations and faiths have been stunned by the amount of violence which has occurred in the first decade of the 21st century. The phenomenon of inter-faith and sectarian warfare has eroded belief in religion as a source of peace and goodwill. When religion becomes the fuel to ignite acts of war and violence, pressure is brought to bear on all faiths to re-examine in depth what it is about religion that allows devout adherents to ignore the goals of peace which are articulated in most religious teachings.

In February 2001, the World Council of Churches launched the *Decade to Overcome Violence: Churches seeking Reconciliation and Peace*. The aim of this decade was to foster a *culture of peace* in opposition to the prevailing culture of violence. It was stated that any justification of war and violence must, to some degree, negate the Christian belief in Jesus Christ as a harbinger of peace and goodwill. I am convinced that gender balance could to some extent reduce the occurrence of acts of violence as the majority of such atrocities are planned and perpetrated by men, though innocent women and children are often the victims of such violence.

In the final chapter of this book, I speculate on how Christianity might best restructure itself so that it is more in touch with the mindset of the times in which it operates.

Like many other Christians, I would like to see our faith remain a positive influence in society. The onus will be on church hierarchies to operate in more flexible ways, rather than being protective of traditions and doctrines that were ethically flawed in the first place.

The target of most church leaders today is to fill parishes with young adults. However, it would appear that less emphasis is being placed on carrying out the myriad of theological, liturgical and scriptural revisions vital for ridding Christianity of inbuilt prejudices. If churches fail to provide an ethical, affirming habitat for all their members, then they will not be an adequate instrument of God's beneficial purpose in the world.

1
A New Millennium Dawns

In 1999, speculation about the survival of mainstream Christianity and of religion *per se* was being aired, becoming a topic for seminars and conferences. I remember there were two brochures sitting on my desk. One advertised a public lecture to be given by Professor Wayne Hudson of Griffith University, Brisbane, on the subject 'The Horizon of Post Religion'. The second brochure gave details of a conference organised by the Australian Association of Studies in Religion on the theme 'The End of Religions? Religion in an Age of Globalisation'. These titles suggested that either religion was dying out or else that, in a global situation where people from different religions and cultures were interacting more closely, traditional forms of belief might need revision. Though millennial celebrations are past history, changes in attitudes and perceptions that may be associated with that event persist and develop as the millennium continues.

Most mainstream Christian churches retain strong links with the ancient worldviews of the centuries in which their scriptures were written and their doctrinal bases formulated. This clinging on to past beliefs, while inspiring for many Christians, can also create difficulties for people living in the 21st century. The basic creeds and theologies still in use in the major denominations were formulated so far back in time that they no longer accord with present understanding of the world we live in. The failure of Christian leaders to loosen the fetters of antiquity as new discoveries concerning the nature of the universe and human development emerge, has led to an exit of younger members from churches.

The dawn of a new millennium might have been an ideal time for mainstream Christianity to start a process of ecclesial spring-cleaning and up-dating. In 1999, there was a global perception that the arrival of the Third Millennium was a significant occasion. Television networks and other media outlets organised link-ups around the world to provide a live cultural kaleidoscope, recording how people of differing nations greeted the 21st century as the clocks reached midnight in their time zones, beginning in the Pacific region. Although not specifically a religious initiative, the link-up developed a spiritual dimension of its own, stressing the aim of love and harmony. For Christians, this theme was pertinent, as in Luke's Gospel account, Jesus' birth had been heralded by a message of peace and goodwill to all people.

Many Christian leaders spoke out strongly on social justice issues as the Third Millennium approached, drawing attention to Jesus Christ's directive to care for the disadvantaged. The year 2000 was declared to be a year in which special consideration should be given to relieving the plight of the increasing number of impoverished people in the world. Christians of various denominations approached governments and loan agencies in the wealthier nations to see if they would write off or restructure the burden of debt which prevented Third World countries, many of which were former European colonies, from developing healthy, stable economies. Unfortunately, the responses were inadequate to meet the need. Poverty remains a major issue today in much of our planet.

Mainstream Christianity noticeably lost ground in the post-World War II period, perhaps because its leaders were seen to be insufficiently critical about warfare as a method of solving global altercations. In 1948, concerned Christians, both ordained and lay, met in Amsterdam to address the problems that faced a world torn apart by major conflict. Those present were aware of the need to create a Christian forum mirroring the recently established United Nations Organisation. The World Council of Churches (WCC) was inaugurated at this meeting, with aims of promoting Christian unity in diversity, peace and justice. Following the use of nuclear bombs against Japan in 1945, there was considerable concern about the development of new weapons capable of inflicting mass destruction on the planet. Christians believed they should in unison exert as much influence as they could to offset such life-destroying, polluting forces.

Since its inception, the WCC has produced in-depth articles and books on how churches might respond to events in the secular arena, stressing the need for peace and justice. The WCC has also organised periodic assemblies of Christians, including the assembly in Brazil in 2006. The reality, however, is that the WCC has not succeeded as much as it hoped in its intent to re-energise Christianity, despite its worthy aims and endeavours. Perhaps the WCC has been too elitist, too remote from grassroots Christians, and too bound to traditional ecclesial structures to achieve its vision. Nor has it ever managed to persuade the Roman Catholic Church, the oldest and largest Christian denomination, to become a member. The Roman Catholic Church today dialogues more closely with the WCC in forums but has not yet become a formal member.

The 'grassroots' has always been an important arena for religious transformation, as the life of Jesus Christ illustrated. Religious hierarchies have a tendency to conserve, rather than modify their basic structures and beliefs. In the 1960s, young people at the grassroots of many nations were in a particularly anti-establishment frame of mind. The radical proclivity of this period was influential in introducing innovations into the religious landscape, at the same time achieving greater acceptance of religious diversity. For example, the Age of Aquarius movement of the 1960s was notable for inculcating a disrespect among youth, in particular for the value systems of Western society, which included a rejection of long-established church attitudes to and rulings on sexual behaviour.

Research studies indicate that churchwomen have consistently constituted the majority group in church communities, despite their subordinate status structurally. Churchwomen's groups have been pressing for more meaningful church roles for women since the end of the nineteenth century. By the late sixties, the voices of churchwomen were growing more insistent, calling for a direct voice at the top-level of church affairs. Churchwomen were outraged when realising that a particularly virulent strain of sexism was institutionalised in the ecclesial systems in which they had spent so much of their life and to which they had given so much of their devotion, faith and energies. The inevitable questions ensued: Would a God of Justice demand that sexual inequality be part of his/her domain? Had religious patriarchy been instituted by churchmen to suit their power aspirations and to accord with the systems prevailing in the secular world? For those who believed that past patriarchs were responsible for the gender imbalance, the immediate task was, with God's help, to rid Christianity of its male hegemonic culture.

Women's spirituality groups on the fringes of mainstream religion mushroomed in the closing years of the second millennium, fuelled by women's awakening to the second-class religious status accorded to them, particularly in the major denominations. Dr Angela Coco, an Australian academic who has researched women's informal Christian groups, discovered that these new associations could be 'found in every religious tradition and culture as well as in groups and organisations separated from traditions'. Coco observed that 'increasingly women are participating in groups which challenge masculinist images of the religious cosmos'.[3]

---

[3] Angela Coco, 'Searching for Reflection: Women's paths to a feminist pagan spirituality group' in *Australian Religious Studies Review*, Vol. 14, Autumn, 2001, p. 20.

Coco found that the majority of women who participated in feminist religious movements had grown up in mainstream Christianity. Most of them had dropped out of their churches, because of being disillusioned by the negative attitudes towards women which they encountered. It was difficult for women to experience spiritual fulfilment in a worshipping environment in which the female perspective was counter-cultural. A noticeable element in women's fringe groups was a desire to confirm that they did have significance in the sight of God. In mainstream Christianity, the messages being relayed to women were that they were marginal, subordinate and, in terms of the generic language and ethos of Scripture and liturgy, invisible as individuals.

Sadly, not all new religious movements promoted freedom, gender balance and justice. Dr Lynne Hume of the University of Queensland found in her research on such movements that 'they vary from those that are almost indistinguishable from mainstream religious groups to those that are highly coercive, totalistic, and demand absolute obedience to a leader'.[4] Being involved in exploitive religious groups has been mostly deleterious for those women and men who are seeking spiritual fulfilment. Cults which attract escapees from the religious mainstream can turn out to be both lacking in spiritual depth and loving kindness. Charismatic leaders, motivated by power ambitions, can exercise very strong social, psychological, sexual and fiscal

---

[4] Lynne Hume, 'New Religious Movements: current research in Australia' in *Australian Religious Studies Review*, Vol. 13, NO. 1, Autumn 2000, p. 27.

control over their adherents, with no regulatory processes to curb their excesses.

Professor Philip Almond, while head of the Department of Philosophy and Religious Studies at the University of Queensland, studied the rise of New Age phenomena, especially those groups surfacing in the second half of the twentieth century. He commented:

> Should we rejoice in it as a new Reformation, rekindling the fires of spirituality for so long dampened by the technological rationalism of the modern industrialised West? Is it a continuation of the counter-culture of the '60s with its (pretended?) rejection of bourgeois culture, or the ultimate in the capitalist commodification of spirituality, or both? There can be little doubt that the New Age is playing a significant role in the construction of late twentieth century Western mentalities.[5]

Almond pointed out that, for some New Agers, 'the cultural weight of the end of a millennium plays a large role'. He observed that, as far as God remains part of the rhetoric of the New Age, 'it is of a being essentially non-interventionist, immanent within rather than transcendent to the world, conceived both impersonally (as, for example, Being itself) and personally, and in the latter case as both male and female'.

---

[5] Philip C. Almond, 'Towards an Understanding of the New Age'. In *Australian Religious Studies Review*, Vol. 6. No.2, Spring, 1993, p. 2.

Almond's remarks were to some extent echoed by front-runners in mainstream Christian theology, an example being the former Episcopal Bishop of Newark, John Shelby Spong, whose book *Why Christianity Must Change or Die* highlighted the need for Christian restructuring. Spong admitted that he, along with many other Christians, was in a state of exile from traditional beliefs because so many of them were based on assumptions about the nature of the planet made in the Bible, which have been invalidated by modern research:

> As Christian history unfolded, the power of the Church to control knowledge and public opinion increased exponentially, and so views of God as both an external power and an invasive deity became dominant in all of Western civilisation. But when the modern age began to dawn, a new understanding of the shape of the universe began to grow and God's place as the heavenly director of human affairs began to totter.[6]

Spong insists that this does not mean that God is non-existent. He claims that he personally communicates with God every day of his life. Spong, however, no longer accepts theism. Theism is the widely held belief in a supernatural deity – God – who is not only the creator of the Universe, but whose power is so comprehensive that God is in total control of everything that occurs in it. Spong sees theism as 'but one human definition of God'. 'The attributes we have

---

[6] Cited in J. S. Spong, *Why Christianity Must Change or Die: a Bishop speaks to Believers in Exile*, Harper, San Francisco, 1998, p. 31.

claimed for God are nothing but human qualities expanded beyond human limits':

> There is no God external to life. God, rather, is the inescapable depth and centre of all that is... God is the Ground of Being itself... The artefacts of the faith of the past must be understood in a new way if they are to accompany us beyond the exile.[7]

Spong believes a non-theistic view of Jesus Christ will make him more believable to generations living in the Third Millennium. He points out that the Gospels were not written to be interpreted literally, nor are they the words of eyewitnesses.

Spong also drew attention to the need for today's Christians to be more environmentally aware, and more accepting of the mounting data on the evolution of the human species over millions of years. At the same time, Spong is fiercely critical of the Creation Science doctrines so popular with fundamentalists, declaring:

> We were not created in God's image in any literal way. We simply evolved out of lower forms of life and ultimately developed a higher consciousness. There is also ample reason today to believe that the species of life known as *Homo sapiens* is not eternal. We have fouled our environmental nest so thoroughly, we have overpopulated our world so irresponsibly, and

---

[7] *Ibid.*, p.70.

we have developed weapons of mass destruction so totally that human survival faces, at best, long odds. We human beings appear to be incidental, both to the past life and to the future life of this planet.[8]

The God portrayed in much of Scripture, and in mainstream Christian creeds and doctrinal statements, is theistic – an almighty, all-knowing super Spirit who is capable of fixing and managing everything that occurs in the Universe. God, while resident above the Earth in Heaven, was believed to intervene constantly in earthly affairs, from solving domestic crises to lending support to nations engaged in warfare. People tended to assume that God was on the side of the victor, an assumption which not only condoned political exploitation of vulnerable peoples but sanctioned colonialism as a form of Godly evangelism.

The theistic concept of God was believable in the first millennium and in a major part of the second, when the Universe was envisioned as a much smaller entity. As space probes and more sophisticated technological and scientific research continue to reveal much more detailed information about the vastness and nature of the Universe, theism loses credibility. Nowadays, it is harder to believe that God is in total control of weather patterns and natural phenomena in the whole Universe, while at the same time attending to the personal needs and requests of every person on earth. People once believed that sickness and pain were God's punishment for sinfulness. Medical research reveals that

---

[8] Ibid., p. 97.

illness or disability is not related to loss of God's favour. Ill-heath occurs because of factors such as viruses, bacteria, malnutrition, body injuries and dysfunctional organs.

Viewpoints such as Spong's are representative of the theological and doctrinal reformation which is occurring within liberal sections of mainstream Christianity. If these new theological viewpoints are to be adopted as orthodoxy, church leaders will require to carry out a major revision of creeds and traditional doctrines. Undoubtedly, for many Christians, it is threatening to move away from the long-held belief in an imperialist Father God, who is capable of controlling everything which is happening in the universe. Yet, in reality, most believers experience God as a beneficial force within, acting like a spiritual director and soul-mate, who nurtures and sustains in a mysterious way. This personal God is more approachable than the theologically constructed monarchical God of creeds and scripture. A non-theistic God is, in many ways, more in harmony with Jesus Christ's reflection of a caring God, for whom the themes of justice and peace were more important than revenge, suffering and militancy. The non-theistic view of God, one could claim, is part of a new age for Christianity, one based on a worldview radically different from that of the first century.

One could argue that all religious faith is evolutionary, that it loses spiritual force if it remains static. Nor is it possible to make an absolute divide between Christianity and the folk religions which it replaced. Christianity, as it evolved, has incorporated pagan ideas and practices into its doctrines and traditions, drawing especially from ancient Mediterranean religions and philosophies. Christianity, as it spread into Europe, timed its religious festivals to coincide with European pagan customs. Christmastide is celebrated at the time of the Winter Solstice, when the Northern Hemisphere is darkest and the light is due to return. The much-loved customs of excessive eating and drinking and the exchange of gifts at this time have been retained and adapted to fit in with the birth stories about Jesus. The fasting period of forty days that precedes Good Friday is known as Lent, an old term for Spring. The word 'Easter' is derived from Eostre, the ancient Spring Goddess of Northern Europe. In pre-Christian Europe, Spring was a time for celebrating the return of life. Of course, for Christians living in the Southern Hemisphere, Christmas and Easter are seasonally out of phase with the North, being celebrated in Summer and Autumn.

Christianity evolved in a milieu where the cultures, beliefs and philosophies of Greece and Rome had widespread religious significance. The New Testament writers, as they tried to capture the essential Gospel, were not only influenced by their Jewish traditions but also had absorbed, to a considerable degree, the dualistic world view of the Greek philosophers. The male body was perceived to be more perfect than that of the female, and men were presumed to be more divine than women. Plato and Pythagoras believed that the human soul was immortal, but also believed that there would be rewards and punishments in the afterlife. These concepts can be found in Old and New Testament eschatological texts, relating to Heaven and Hell.

The Graeco-Roman heritage in Christianity is still influential today, perhaps because of its strong legitimisation of patriarchy. In his encyclical *Fides et Ratio* [Faith and

Reason], published in October 1998, Pope John Paul II warned that 'the Graeco-Latin heritage must not be abandoned by theologians engaging with Eastern cultures', declaring: 'In engaging great cultures for the first time, the Church cannot abandon what she has gained from her inculturation in the world of Graeco-Latin thought'.[9] Yet, for Christian women, these philosophies have left a bitter legacy of sexual discrimination and violence, which has continued on into the Third Millennium. It must also be noted that Graeco-Roman philosophies were developed within a pantheistic religious milieu, which did not fit comfortably with the monotheism of Judaeo-Christian belief or with the non-discriminatory ethos modelled by Jesus Christ.

In Roman Catholicism, women in religious orders were also influenced by the feminist and justice movements of the sixties. In Roman Catholicism and Eastern Orthodoxy, major decision-making is restricted to males in ordained ministry. All Roman Catholic priests and most senior Orthodox clergy are celibate, thus even more accustomed to living and working in a male enclave. However, as more women religious were allowed by their superiors to take university courses, so that they could obtain the tertiary qualifications required for their educational, social and medical work, they began to respond to the radical currents circulating on campuses.

The greater freedoms allowed to Catholic nuns by the Second Vatican Council in the 1960s were interpreted as a sanction for women religious to participate more fully in

---

[9] Cited in *Church Times*, 16 October 1998.

general Catholic affairs, including policy making. When the conservative church leaders who succeeded Pope John XXIII tried to curb the liberating forces released by the Second Vatican Council, they discovered that many Catholic nuns had progressed too far from the cloistered past to accept retrogression.

Women religious occupied an intriguing position as potential agents for change. Although they did not occupy the corridors of direct power in church or society, they did enjoy a degree of autonomy (ecclesial and financial). When they too began to challenge the church establishment, they could do so from the position of having a strong community with resources to back them. For many women religious, their liberation from the restrictions of the past became a source of new understandings of God, self, church, community and the world.

Not all those leaving their churches pursued the path of reformation. There was also a rekindled interest in paganism within some of the new religious movements, with assertions that this old religion was not as totally evil as people were taught to believe during the Christianisation process in Europe. Neo-paganism today has much in common with eco-spirituality and, according to Graham St. John in his studies of this phenomenon, results from 'a growing discontent with what are revealed to be the strong anthropocentric and patriarchal foundations of Western Science and Judeo-Christianity'. St. John quotes as follows from T. Luhrmann's article 'The Resurgence of Romanticism: Neo-Paganism, Feminist Spirituality, and the Divinity of Nature' in his work *Environmentalism*:

> There is no god, masculine, separate and transcendentally aloof, but rather an ancient divinity immanent in the world...The natural landscape becomes a map for human feeling and aspiration, an environment for spiritual odyssey.[10]

A marked difference between Christians and neo-pagans is the latter's lack of 'hang-ups' about the basic sinfulness of the human body. Neo-pagans have less moral apprehensions about sexuality and affinity with the natural world.

As noted previously, belief systems tend to be influenced by the religious philosophies of each passing age. The increasing globalisation of communities has resulted in the phenomenon of Eastern religions impinging on Christianity, and Christianity becoming popular in many parts of Asia and the Pacific region. Christians nowadays perceive that there are benefits in learning spiritual skills, such as meditation, from other faiths, especially Buddhism and Hinduism, in order to deepen their own spirituality.

The dilemma facing Christians in the Third Millennium is whether to preserve the past or carry out major reconstruction in order to present Christianity to oncoming generations in a more up-to-date form. Dr Noel Preston, a senior minister in the Uniting Church in Australia, confesses that for most of his adult years he has questioned certain dogmas 'which are sometimes defended by theological

---

[10] T. Luhrmann, 'The resurgence of romanticism, contemporary neopaganism, feminist spirituality and the divinity of nature' in K. Milton (ed.) *Environmentalism*, Routledge, London, pp. 219-232.

double-talk'. He admits the ancient creeds 'do not express what he believes very well' and at times 'he has almost choked on the words of some hymns'.[11] Preston considers that religions, as a human construct, 'audaciously claim authority over Truth, and the power of franchisees of the divine, a power which can so easily corrupt'. Dr Preston believes Christianity can be a good and positive force, drawing attention to the beneficial contributions Christians have made for humankind. 'Institutional religion has been the crucible from which many worthwhile community service programs emanate and through which millions of individuals find inspiration and solace.'

Conservative Christian leaders, when challenged to carry out reforms, can resist vigorously. They especially reject suggestions that female as well as male metaphors are suitable for God, despite the fact that the Bible states that both men and women are made in God's image. Traditionalists tend to romanticise their religious past. They react protectively when challenged to jettison conceptual forms which were never relevant in the domain of a God of love and equity, but which did reflect the hierarchical structures of human feudal societies. Church leaders accuse their critics of trying to remodel God's kingdom to fit the *Zeitgeist*, the Spirit of the Age. They ignore the fact that, after two thousand years, their world view might be riddled with elements of supernatural fantasy, which were acceptable truths in the first millennium, but are no longer believable in the third.

---

[11] Cited in *Courier Mail*, 1 April 2002.

The lay people who remain in mainstream parishes tend to be those who cherish the familiar worship forms, which they have experienced throughout their lives. Church attendance is regarded as the most effective way of keeping in touch with God. Many Christians believe their religious priority should be to belong to a Christian group, which is dedicated to spreading the Gospel of Jesus Christ. Regular churchgoers also value being part of a close-knit community, where they have built up friendships. Most consider that the Bible, being categorised in liturgies as 'the Word of God', still conveys important messages for today's people.

However, the reality today is that there is a dearth of young parents and children in many church congregations. Sunday schools have reduced numbers because the children's parents no longer feel sufficiently motivated to go to church. Young parents busily engage in non-church activities at weekends, especially mothers who combine a career with household management. Men nowadays are more attracted to recreational activities with families or mates on the weekend as a break from the pressures of the working week. Yet, despite the lack of people's involvement in church activities, surveys show that a high level of belief in God remains in society generally. In times of danger or stress, people find comfort in prayer, even though they have ceased to have a church affiliation.

As church attendance declines, Christian leaders lose their influence over secular affairs. Church affiliation becomes even more a private affair, with clergy's public role mainly being to act as consultants when moral dilemmas occur or to carry out rites of passage, such as baptisms, weddings and funerals. Church attendance has ceased to have the customary significance it had in the nineteenth and early twentieth century. As one young Australian replied when the minister of his local Uniting Church asked him why he had left the congregation, 'You know how it is, Rev, churchgoing is no longer "cool"'.

For many traditional churchgoers, the word 'cool' is threatening because it has connotations of a 'pop' culture, which they regard as irreverent, blasphemous and sensual, undermining core Christian moral values. The problem for Christian institutions is how to achieve a balance between 'secular coolness' and 'church teaching'. Attempts to discard familiar but hopelessly outmoded forms of liturgy, hymns and biblical interpretation can meet with strong opposition from those who make up the majority of today's congregations – the 'over-fifties'. The use of rock bands and more modern music in church services does, to some degree, act as a draw card, particularly to younger people. The downside is that many of the lyrics are still based on outdated doctrines where metaphors for God are monarchical, feudal or overly paternal.

Church leaders and lay members have been alarmed by the continuing loss of human and financial resources to carry out their ministry. In the past, mainstream churches survived periods of decline through state aid, good investment management and tax concessions. Today, churches mainly receive state aid for the management of social welfare projects and schools. For general parish maintenance, the majority of churches depend heavily on the income their parishioners provide. The most common response to calls for reform is for senior church leaders to set up councils and committees to advise on what paradigm shifts they ought or are prepared to make. Such bodies tend to be made up of church members who favour the status quo and are reluctant to make major changes.

The rise of fundamentalism within Christianity is to some extent a response to the fear of losing the safe certainty of biblical absolutism, the belief the Bible is literally the 'Word of God'. In fundamentalism, the Bible becomes the supreme tangible reality. Fundamentalists fiercely reject modern theological concepts and are suspicious of the findings of modern research on how the Bible's contents were collated and written. They resent the inroads such research has made on the credibility of the Bible as history, especially disliking terms such as metaphor, symbol and myth. Fundamentalists are reluctant to accept that Scripture more often reveals God indirectly through human interpretation, images and allegories. Outwardly, fundamentalist churches have popular appeal, because they don a facade of modernism, using the music and presentation style of pop culture. But underneath the 'hype' lurks a very inflexible puritan piety based on literal interpretations of Scripture, which are absurd in the light of scientific evidence concerning the nature of the Earth and its place in the universe. For women, fundamentalism may offer the security of absolutism but it also embraces a doctrine of female subordination.

In societies where the deconstruction of the myths and stereotypes of the past are not always replaced by socially beneficial belief systems, people become confused and unsettled. They are attracted to the fundamentalist right or to charismatic leaders who promise that, in return for total obedience to their particular religious group, they will reach heaven. As Riane Eisler warns in her work *Sacred Pleasure*:

Certainly, if the fundamentalist right succeeds in seizing power, we will see extreme social and sexual controls. For what they would impose on us is a religious form of fascism in which the ultimate strongman is a wrathful divine father who countenances neither freedom nor equality, whose power – like that of the men who rule in his name – is imposed and maintained through threats (and intermittent acts) of the most painful violence.[12]

So, in the first decade of the 21st century, Christian churches are confused, suffering a lack of confidence and a shortage of members and funds. There are tensions between the religious 'Old Age' and the 'New Age', between conservative Christians and the reformers, and between reformers and the post-Christians. This religious upheaval is creating a dynamic situation which is both destructive and conducive to new life. What the majority of Christian leaders of the mainstream, fundamentalist and Pentecostal churches fail to articulate is that perhaps the most urgent reform needed throughout Christianity is to achieve gender balance, not just by allowing women into top leadership roles, but by examining all doctrines, scriptures, sacraments, symbols and structures that exclude women or suggest that they are not as important human beings as are men. The ultimate challenge for churchmen – and especially clergy – is to be prepared to share with women the privileged status churches have bestowed upon them.

---

[12] Riane Eisler, *Sacred Pleasure: Sex, Myth and the Politics of the Body*, Doubleday, Sydney, p. 199.

2

Christianity's Credibility Crisis

As observed in the previous chapter, religion is not a spent force in the Third Millennium. The multiplicity of religious movements emerging globally is a sign that people still value having a spiritual dimension in their lives. Religion usually represents a more transcendental aspect of life, contrasting with the technologically-advanced, materially-driven milieu that dominates so much of global perspectives. Many people, despite the present emphasis on worldliness, find comfort in the Christian belief that there exists a caring, powerful force for good, a supreme spirit who is absolutely trustworthy and capable of achieving favourable outcomes in times of trauma and ordeal.

In today's Western Christian communities, research figures show that fewer people attend mainstream Christian churches regularly than in the past. The vacuum is not just being filled by new religious movements offering alternative forms of worship. The void is providing new opportunities for atheists to put forward what they consider to be the basic reasons for the decline in Christianity's heartland. One of the main conclusions reached by religious sceptics is that important elements of Christian Scripture and doctrine contradict natural law and scientific knowledge of the universe, and thus no longer have credibility.

Atheist writers such as Richard Dawkins in his book *The God Delusion* and Christopher Hitchens in his work *God is not Great: Religion Poisons Everything*, claim that religion, whether it be tolerant or extremist, is not wholesome because the demands of religious belief defy reason, thus becoming a source of ignorance, prejudice and violence. In terms of sexuality, atheists see believers in God as kill-joys, and especially repressive of women.

Atheists have long targeted religion, and especially Christianity, as seen in the rise of Communism in the 20th century. Yet, despite the draconian assaults on religious worship in communist countries, such as in the Soviet bloc and China, the major faiths have sprung back into popularity once the restraints were removed or eased. The Eastern Orthodox Churches have experienced strong revival in former Soviet states and Christianity is allowed much greater freedom in China, despite the country still adopting a communist form of government.

The renaissance of Christianity in Eastern Europe is particularly encouraging for those who believe that Christianity can survive, despite the appearance of new religious movements in its heartland. Clearly, the onus now rests on mainstream Christian leaders to be sufficiently daring and innovative in their response to the challenges of the new millennium. Nor will it be sufficient to argue the case for retaining outdated theology and doctrines, especially those which discriminate against women. Christian leaders need to accept that the roles formerly reserved for males should now be open to females, not because of feminist pressure but because Jesus Christ never declared that women followers were inferiors in his religious movement. He encouraged them to spread his message in their communities.

The present pattern of church attendance indicates that there is a growing shortage of women in congregations with the time, physical fitness or inclination to carry out the domestic chores expected of them in the past. Nor can clergy assume that their flock will contain a sizeable number of young mothers and children to fill the spaces left when elderly parishioners pass on. The statistics from religious surveys indicate that twenty-first century women are quietly but firmly rejecting acceptance of an ancient, overwhelmingly patriarchal ethos as a basis of belief. When young women cease to be church members, there is a tendency for children and spouses to drop out too. Although the gender bias in Christianity favours masculinity, lay males tend not to attend church unless their wives/partners and children are present with them.

There is today an urgent need for church leaders to undertake major reform if they are serious about setting Christianity on the road towards regeneration. In the present world, where diverse cultures are interacting with each other far more than in the past, one cannot assume that the majority of Westernised people are affiliated with mainstream Christianity. Christian churches are operating in a pluralist religious marketplace, where there is diminishing public concern about what religion a person embraces, as long as its followers behave in a socially acceptable and lawful manner. Nevertheless, Christianity's long-standing eminence in European culture gives it an advantage over other faith systems in the west. It is now up to church leaders to acknowledge that mainstream Christianity is losing touch with the younger generations living in the Third Millennium. Spiritual vibrancy is more noticeable on the fringes of faith systems.

Certainly, the core message promulgated by Christian leaders has been to draw people closer to God through following the example of Jesus Christ. The Gospels depict Jesus Christ as a person with selfless concern for others, especially the disadvantaged. That Jesus was willing to sacrifice his life for his ideals still has very special religious significance for a diverse range of people. One of Jesus' customs, recorded especially in the Gospel of Luke, was to encourage women to take active ministry roles in the Jesus movement, a radical deviation from the norm in the Mediterranean region in which Jesus lived. One of the failings of the Christian faith that evolved in the centuries following Jesus' crucifixion, was the gradual removal of women from leadership positions in the church. Early Christianity began in house churches, based on a surprisingly egalitarian culture. When organised Christianity stopped being persecuted and instead was elevated to being the established religion of the Roman imperial system, the egalitarian culture of the earliest Christian churches was replaced by the patriarchal structures of the political system which they served. Today, church leaders – if they are to be true to Jesus' example – will need sufficient flexibility and patience to tune into the spiritual needs of people of differing generations, sexes and traditions. Worship patterns in mainstream parishes have been undergoing considerable changes, geared towards making churchgoing more appealing to youth, but often without success in halting the exodus of the younger generations. The reality for church leaders is that superficial alterations have not stemmed the drop-out rate of church members. The reform processes need to venture into those deep, ecclesial places so often declared to be too sacred to change.

One of these areas involves the nature of the relationship between clergy and the divine, which in turn will require scrutiny of the traditional division between ordained and lay Christians and whether this honorary divinity accorded to male clergy in particular, accords with Jesus' ideal of a priesthood of all believers. Despite the reality of predominately grey-haired worshippers scattered around the pews, church leaders are reluctant to admit openly that the majority of their membership is made up of those who are nearing the end of their lives. Elderly churchgoers tend to prefer retaining the status quo, seeing themselves as upholders of Christian morals in the midst of an increasingly secular society. The majority of today's practising Christians have been law-abiding and charitable people, believing that propriety is a necessary factor for carrying out God's will.

Older churchgoers are disturbed by the reality that their adult children, who were brought up to pray to God and read the Bible regularly, currently attend church infrequently or not at all. They worry about their grandchildren as they perceive them growing up in an environment where Christian teaching is sketchy and church attendance sporadic. Liberal attitudes to sex and unmarried partnerships also concern older Christians, who have been taught to regard promiscuity and marital breakdown as being particularly sinful.

Younger Christian laity who have retained their church affiliation are becoming increasingly frustrated when they realise that they lack the power to effect the major changes they believe might attract the oncoming generations back to regular worship. The laity, especially in Roman Catholicism and Orthodoxy, has very limited access to the central councils, which legitimise major reforms. Changes in worship do occur at the grassroots level, especially in situations of clergy shortage, but because of the tight legitimising systems in place in major areas of mainstream Christianity, these innovations do not always receive the necessary stamp of approval from the clerical hierarchy. Lay initiatives, especially if instigated by laywomen, are too often dismissed as unworkable or contrary to church law.

Thus, in the mainstream Christian churches, the responsibility for remedial action rests squarely on those in power, predominantly male clergy. A cultural problem within established churches is that hierarchies are by nature conservative. They have a propensity to sidetrack contentious issues, unless the matters raised are receiving excessive adverse comment in the public domain. On the whole, cardinals, bishops, patriarchs and moderators react evasively to complaints that traditional worship is boring, and that the ecclesial system is bogged down in outdated dogma and unacceptable scriptural interpretation.

Senior clergy are certainly aware of inadequacies, as reflected in comments made in March 2006 by the Roman Catholic Archbishop of Brisbane, John Bathersby, who is reputedly a moderate prelate. When questioned about declining numbers of priests and laity, the Archbishop replied:

> We've got to get out there, we've got to help the poor and needy but we need to do so with the vision of Christ, with that deeper dimension of being linked to God, to all people, to all creation. I think this vision is...sellable. But we can't get it out...we're to blame too. For the fact is the church gets in the way. People look and they say there's no life, no vitality there.[13]

It is interesting that, in this interview, Archbishop Bathersby evaded a suggestion that the ordination of women to priesthood might relieve the shortage of male priests, at the same time effecting a modicum of gender balance. He did, however, admit that when people refer to the pre-Second Vatican Council period as 'the good old days', he becomes depressed.

Traditional Church doctrines, including ethics, are increasingly viewed as being too remote from the reality of life in the modern world, especially in the fields of theology, ecology, sociology and biotechnology. In too many instances, church traditions and rulings are perceived as being below the moral standards in place in secular society.

---

[13] Cited in *Courier Mail*, Brisbane, 5 March 2006.

For example, discrimination, in terms of gender, class and age, is declared to be unacceptable under various United Nations and national charters on human rights. Thus, for disenchanted Christians, especially women, church systems which are based on the ranking of man over woman, ordained man over layman, and humankind over nature are today viewed as seriously flawed.

While Christianity's mainstream heartland declines, the interesting phenomenon is that those regions where Christianity took root under the aegis of colonialism are the areas where church numbers are increasing rather than declining. As a result, the centre of gravity of Christianity is shifting from the West to places such as Latin America, Africa, parts of Asia and the Pacific. This shift has led to innovations in worship patterns in these areas, most noticeably the incorporation of elements of indigenous culture and belief. The national, denominational and churchmanship factors, which marred the Christian message exported by European missionaries, are being critiqued by post-colonial indigenous religious leaders. They recognise that these introduced denominational divisions fractured indigenous societies.

Western missionaries had a Christian duty to be a force for peace and reconciliation, but the record shows that their evangelism was tainted by denominational and imperialist loyalties. These factors engendered unseemly competitiveness in their attempts to capture the souls of the indigenous peoples. European missionaries, perhaps unwittingly, also projected attitudes of white racial superiority, as well as sanctifying religious patriarchy, to the detriment of the local women. Most indigenous women needed liberation from male domination rather than its ratification. Thus, Jesus' message was distorted by church practice, preventing the gentle blending of Christianity into native cultures to transform them from within.

Karimi Kinoti, a Methodist theologian from Kenya, has written on the church's failure to improve attitudes towards women, commenting that she had recently asked a clergyman why the church in Kenya remained conspicuously silent on the problem of violence against women. Kinoti is convinced that:

> If the numerous stories and statistics presented of women who are killed by their spouses, battered, raped and violated in many other ways around the world does not prick the conscience of the church, then one must conclude that we are faced with a deep ethical and moral crisis. That the churches should be selective in their understanding of violence, their mission for social justice and their witness to the marginalised is a serious indictment of their credibility.[14]

Religious restructuring in post-colonial nations is, to a large extent, motivated by a strong desire for freedom from European cultural dominance. There is a fierce determination in new African nations to restore credibility and dignity to indigenous culture, with the formation of

---

[14] Karimi Kinoti, 'Overcoming Violence: Taking a Gender Perspective' in *The Ecumenical Review*, Vol. 55, No. 3, July 2003, p. 226.

splinter Christian churches, which prefer to be independent rather than remain linked to Western denominations. These changes do not always benefit women, especially those living in economic impoverishment. In both Western and postcolonial Christianity, strong patriarchal attitudes remain part of the ecclesial system. It is now the task of indigenous Christian women, especially those who have gained status through education, to strive to challenge religious practices that disadvantage women. Their contribution will be particularly important while religious restructuring processes are taking place.

The demise of political colonialism was bound to cause global unrest because the colonisers departed leaving their subjects without a just model of government to emulate, and without the economic resources to lift the standard of living of the people. The centralist dominator model of rule adopted by European colonisers replaced less tightly structured indigenous tribal rule. It has been difficult for newly independent nations, with limited resources, to formulate a system of government able to cater for the needs of all the people. As a consequence of this, the governing systems in place tend to enrich those who gained political power through control of the military forces.

Western imperialism has enduring roots; its vestiges remain in the majority of postcolonial nations. This neocolonialism is economic rather than political, with newly emerging nations oppressed by the overwhelming debt they owe to overseas financial agencies. The wealth of most developing nations is being syphoned off to repay interest on loans or to enrich corrupt national elites. As a result, there is a large percentage of powerless, starving people who live below the poverty line, in post-colonial nations. There is recognition that Western Christianity's immediate task is to help the impoverished peoples of the world to become self-sufficient by being prepared to share their wealth with them without expecting an economic return. Achieving this aim is hampered by the reality that Western Christianity itself is in decline.

Pressure for restructuring is a global phenomenon, especially in post-colonial nations and areas where governments are unstable or overly despotic. People who feel oppressed periodically take to the streets, demanding a more democratic system of rule, and an end to endemic political corruption so that the national economy benefits all the population rather than an elitist minority. In Malaysia, for example, the word displayed a few years ago on the banners raised aloft by activists was *'Reformasi'*, meaning reformation.

Reformation is a concept with which Christians are familiar. It was the term used to denote the major break in the Middle Ages within the Roman Catholic Church. In the 1300s and 1400s, demands for reform began to surface, becoming more strident when no remedial action was taken. Northern Europeans in particular resented the abuses which had crept into the administration and organisation of the Rome-centred Church. They perceived a decline in clergy morality, especially among those in higher orders. Reformers believed they had the right to communicate with their God directly rather than through a priest.

Church and state interacted so closely in the Middle Ages that changes in the secular world inevitably affected religious institutions. Feudal societal structures had begun to loosen, forced to adapt to the growth of wealthy middle classes, whose economic power challenged the autocracy of the princes of the state. As is the case today, there were important social, political and economic factors, which impinged on the religious as well as the state establishments, sparking demands for change. The breakaway from Roman Catholicism in the Middle Ages was triggered by groups such as the Albigensians in France, climaxing under the leadership of men such as Martin Luther and John Calvin.

In respect to women, the Reformation of the Middle Ages enhanced the respectability of marriage, but did not change the status of women in any significant way. Luther used the Creation story in the second chapter of Genesis as a basis for the earthly subordination of women. The sinfulness of Eve is today still used in many Christian churches as evidence of women's inferior status, despite the acknowledgment by most theologians that the Creation story cannot be taken literally in view of the scientific evidence now available regarding the evolution of homo sapiens over millions of years. Interestingly, Luther also used natural phenomena to support his views about women, stating that 'the male is like the sun in heaven, the female like the moon', claiming that 'just as in all the rest of nature, the strength of the male exceeds that of the female, so also in the perfect nature the male somewhat excelled the female'.[15]

Today, the Roman Catholic Church still has a male-centric structure, but, at the grassroots of the 'diaspora', much more independent patterns of worship and theologising

---

[15] Martin Luther, *Lectures in Genesis*, cited in Margaret M. Miles, *Carnal Knowing*, Vintage Books, New York, 1991, pp. 107-109.

are emerging, with demands for democratisation of the centralised system. As in the former Reformation period, there are calls for improved clergy morality, following revelations of a culture of sexual abuse and paedophilia in clergy ranks across the globe.

The emergence of rebellious movements in Roman Catholicism today differs from the Middle Ages. Many of the prime movers for institutional change are women, including women in religious orders. Patriarchs of the Eastern Orthodox Churches, which separated from Western Christianity in the eleventh century, are also trying to cope with demands for modernisation of their ecclesial systems. Many of their clergy and members suffered and struggled for survival under Communist regimes for most of the twentieth century. In former USSR political entities, Orthodox adherents are rejoicing in the renewed right to worship freely, but the clerical elite is finding it difficult to maintain its autocratic, patriarchal church traditions in the new democracy-seeking cultural environments surrounding them.

In his Report to the World Council of Churches Central Council meeting in 2001, Orthodox Catholicus of Cilicia, Aram I, admitted that 'globalization is imposing new ways of "being church"', affecting even the church's self-understanding:

> The question is 'How do we live our faith in the context of globalization?' What does 'being church' mean in a fenceless society? This is the most acute concern and initial challenge that the churches must wrestle with

in the context of an ecumenical response to globalization. Indeed, globalization questions our narrow ecclesiological perspectives and ossified perceptions and calls us to make a comprehensive and critical assessment of our ecclesiological self-understanding.[16]

Politics, social upheaval, economics and religion have always been a volatile mixture. As the irreverent but astute Australian writer and broadcaster, Phillip Adams, has commented: 'Instead of being the opium of the people, religion is crack cocaine. Which is why it has, for millenniums, ignited crusades, wars and genocide'.[17]

In today's global marketplace, there is a greater focus on free enterprise and individualism but, as we have seen, these two factors are also having an impact on religious institutions. There are pluses and minuses in this for Christians. Among the pluses is a much greater openness about religion *per se*. Christians are daring to query revered doctrines rather than accept passively whatever Church leaders declare to be immutable truths. Among the minuses – as mentioned in the previous chapter – is that individualism can lead to excessive Christian disunity and the formation of dysfunctional cults.

The Christian mainstream is in decline at a time in history when the world desperately needs to hear the message of love and compassion at the core of Jesus'

---

[16] Report of Moderator of the WCC Central Council, 2001, in *The Ecumenical Review*, Vol. 54, No. 4, October 2002, p. 484.
[17] See *Weekend Australian*, 20-21 February 1999.

teachings. Christians, despite their doctrinal and male-centric shortcomings, have performed well in areas of social outreach to the sick, outcast and illiterate, inspired by Jesus' deep concern for those who are despised and rejected. Churches more than ever need young people willing to continue social outreach to the underprivileged. The most serious human problem the world is facing in the twenty-first century is the growing disparity between the rich minority and the poor majority. It is estimated that 20% of the world's population presently live in inhuman circumstances, exacerbated by the spread of AIDS and the lack of funding to provide adequate treatment for sufferers of the disease. There are also too many areas torn apart by war, with religious divisions being exploited to fan the flames of hatred. And the poorest of the poor, and those innocent people who are most often the victims of predominantly male-instigated conflicts, are women and children. The magnitude of atrocities perpetrated against women today is staggering, and is becoming increasingly cruel and life destroying.

In his article on 'Overcoming Globalization: The Root of Violence', Kelly Luwig, the youth secretary of the National Council of Churches in the Philippines, describes how much women are exploited worldwide:

> Traditionally, women workers get hired last and fired first, need to be better qualified... get paid

less than a man for the same job and end up with the most demeaning or repetitive kinds of work.[18]

In his 'Letter to Women' dated 29 June 1995, Pope John Paul II acknowledged that women's dignity had not been respected. 'They have often been relegated to society's margins and even reduced to servitude', which has resulted in 'a spiritual impoverishment of humanity'.[19] However, on the church issue which discriminates against women more than any other, ordination to priesthood, Pope John Paul II remained unmoved, trying to soften his stance by declaring that because 'women are not ordained priests in no way detracts from the role of women, since all share equally in the dignity proper to the "common priesthood"'. 'Common priesthood' used as a euphemism for laity, represents exclusion from major decision-making and top leadership in the Roman Catholic system.

In the years that lie ahead, Christian relief agencies should not only focus on relieving the plight of disadvantaged women but also seek ways to liberate them from structured powerlessness, violent abuse and illiteracy. The Christian men given charge of aid agencies tend to be culturally insensitive to women's special need to be empowered. Leaders of mainstream churches have also paid less attention to the plight of women in mission planning, subsuming them under men's affairs, without identifying the negative effects flowing from women's situation of

---

[18] Kelly Luwig, 'Overcoming Globalization: The Root of Violence', in *The Ecumenical Review*, Vol. 55, No. 3, July 2003, p. 250.

[19] Cited in *Catholic Leader*, 23 July 1995.

inequity. For this deficiency to be remedied, as much weight must be given to women's needs as to those of men, with more women appointed to leadership positions in welfare agencies.

There have been some indications that the voices of women are infiltrating the top echelons of mainstream churches. In Section 2.7 of the Papers for the 1998 Anglican Lambeth Conference, the following statement was made: 'Our willingness to repent and to change is crucial because then others can see that Christian humanity is still a humanity like theirs, fragile and mobile, and that God is always ready to grant us new beginnings'.[20] The Lambeth Papers also conceded that, to achieve the goal of the Church as a model community, it should discern and identify all discriminatory practices in its structures, images and symbols, and commit itself to reform and renewal. The glaring omission in these statements was that the word 'women' was never mentioned.

Freedom to communicate is a basic human right not always endorsed in religious circles. Several Christian leaders have taken action to impose silence in regard to contemporary church issues, such as the papal ban on discourse about the ordination of women. Blanket bans of this kind can backfire. If people are denied the right to express opinions on topics which affect them personally, then inevitably resentment will build up, especially when, as in the case of women, the censorship runs contrary to papal promises to upgrade women's status in the church. When church leaders display double standards in their treatment

---

[20] 'The Lambeth Papers', in *Church Times*, 8 May 1998, p. 16.

of their flock, people begin to query whether the Church is an ethical institution. The ecclesial flaws begin to emerge from the woodwork.

Improved communication networks are enabling human rights movements to support one another to ensure that the voice of the grassroots is heard alongside statements by those in power, including religious leaders. By logging on to http://www.womenpriests.org, for example, one can get access to over 2000 documents in English language relevant to the ordination of women. The director of this website is John Wijngaards, a former Catholic priest, who directs his information service from Rickmansworth in England. According to Wijngaards, 'In order to bring about the necessary reforms in the Church, we need to create new levels of awareness among all members of the Christian community. We believe that the Internet offers marvellous opportunities for this'.

Dafne Plou, an Argentinean journalist, in her studies on global communication, has confirmed that networking has been beneficial for women. According to Plou, 'when the women's movement began organising for the UN World Conference on Population and Development in Cairo in 1994, they used all sorts of communication networks, from group to electronic media, to ensure that their defence of women's rights to reproductive health would not be stifled or side-tracked by debate on the abortion issue'.[21] Plou,

---

[21] Dafne S. Plou, Global Communication: *Is There a Place for Human Dignity?*, Risk Books, Geneva, 1996, p. 62.

however, also expressed her concerns about the Western-based multinational corporations, who control the media and manipulate it for their own economic advantage:

> We must move from a technocracy that rules over people to a humanization of technology placed at the service of individuals and peoples... If the voices of all are to be heard, 'globalization from below' must be strengthened.[22]

The established pattern of church information being disseminated from the top down – from bishop to priest and from priest to parishioner – has been challenged by cyberspace. Internet dialogue, electronic conferencing, and email provide for spontaneous exchanges of ideas among a much wider group of participants. It is more difficult to control dissent and ban theological discourse which takes place outside the accepted parish or diocesan parameters. As Professor David Lochhead observed in his work on information technology and the church, 'computer communication marginalizes hierarchy'.[23]

That church leaders are wary of cyberspace was reflected in the Moderator of the WCC's 2001 Report, when he claimed that 'globalization has created its own system, values, and criteria':

> The global space is an anthropocentric reality, dominated by secularism, syncretism and

---

[22] Ibid., pp. 64-65.
[23] D. Lochhead, *Shifting Realities: Information Technology and the Church*, Risk Books, Geneva, 1997, p. 77.

consumerism. In spite of its tremendous technological, scientific and economic progress and achievement, the space provided by globalization will, sooner or later, become a dangerous place if it is not given a 'moral orientation' and a 'spiritual sustenance'.[24]

This statement ignores the reality that cyberspace has been religiously liberating for women, providing them with opportunities to gain spiritual affirmation of their worth, an element of Christianity which has been noticeably lacking in mainstream churches. The most pressing concern today is that so many of the world's disadvantaged women have no access to computers, nor have the literacy needed to make use of them. Third world women are so engrossed by the daily struggle to survive, that the attainment of gender justice is a luxury they are forced to forego. Yet the reality is that incidents of violence against women are particularly high in poverty-stricken areas. Oppressed women need to be able to tell the world how much they suffer.

Technological progress has always been an important concept in the West. Political and economic supremacy has strong associations with advantage in terms of weaponry, mobility, people control, communications, food production and mineral extraction. However, the alliance of progress, science and technology in the West has had social and religious consequences – good and bad – for technologically disadvantaged ethnic groups. Indigenous people under colonialism were too often categorised as

---

[24] Report of WCC Moderator, p. 492.

lesser human beings because of their failure to develop modern technology. In dualistic Western Christian thought, human beings were considered to be sacred but the rest of the natural world was not. Thus, Christians rationalised the destruction of indigenous peoples on the grounds of their closeness to nature and remoteness from God.

One of the most serious hurdles facing global harmony in the new millennium is this disparity between the rich and the poor, between the developed and the developing countries of the world and between the Northern and Southern hemispheres. The processes of globalisation are not inclusive; they tend to privilege a minority among the world's population. The globalised market tends to ignore the needs of the poor and the market itself becomes almost an idol. Consumerism is the new religion for many people. In the global market, there are insufficient opportunities for cordial human relationships to develop because of the weight accorded to competitiveness. In terms of gender, human relationships cannot improve as long as pejorative evaluations are applied to women and preferential status is attributed to men in everyday discourse.

It would appear that the faster technological, social and economic change takes place, the more those in positions of power take advantage of the situation to extend their interests, creating monopolies that swallow up smaller-scale, local enterprise. Monopolies tend to undermine the processes of self-sufficiency so essential for strengthening developing nations. Third World leaders are at the same time tempted to pour money allocated for grassroots development into the creation of images of modernity in order to overcome the stigma of appearing as representative of former defeated peoples. This is an unfortunate but understandable reaction of people who have endured indignity, genocide and the intentional dismantling of their cultural values.

Inequalities of wealth and power are being challenged by a plethora of grassroots protest groups, aiming to counter the excesses of autocratic rulers. Many of these groups come under the classification 'non-government organisations (NGOs)', such as Amnesty International, Women's Electoral Lobby, Pakistan Association for Women's Studies, Greenpeace, and thousands more. These grassroots movements are particularly concerned with human and civil rights, together with environmental issues. Mainstream Christian denominations are discovering that there are also growing numbers of protest groups forming within their own ranks, bringing pressure for major church reform.

NGOs, through their outspoken criticisms, have forced establishments to ponder on the concepts in their traditional philosophies and doctrines which have damaged rather than enhanced the inhabitants of planet Earth. Respect for God's creation and all people within it, irrespective of race, gender and class, is gaining recognition as a spiritual and theological basis for justice. The social, economic and political upheavals we are observing around the world are not entirely unique to our age. One could argue that Christianity itself grew out of a period of political and religious imbalance.

Jesus' reform movement emerged in the first century in a period when the injustice and oppression of Roman colonialism was making life a struggle for survival for the landless poor. Jesus made it very clear in the first century that the 'Kingdom of God' movement, which he founded, must address socio-political and economic imbalances. Love for God and all other people took precedence. In his Palestinian environment, Jesus was aware that colonial taxes and the self-interest of the elites had reduced the ordinary, powerless citizen to a state of gruelling poverty. One could argue that when Christianity was adopted as the state religion of the Roman Empire, its male hierarchy began a process of backsliding, losing touch with the common people, and especially the disadvantaged, in a fashion quite contrary to Jesus' principles.

Two millennia later, the emphasis on technological advancement has taken its toll on the resources of the planet as well as on human life. Ecological degradation on a massive scale has occurred because of tree clearing, urbanisation, air and land pollution, and an accumulation of harmful waste. According to Matthew Fox, the well-known American Catholic (now Episcopalian) philosopher and theologian, Christians must bear responsibility for this degradation. The West did not develop a theory of God the Creator. If it had done so, Christianity would not have been so blind to Mother Earth. The emphasis in Christianity has been on humans having dominion, rather than stewardship, over the earth and its resources. If God the Creator had been emphasised, 'religion would have named the sins of ecocide and biocide and genocide a long time ago'.[25]

It is not easy to come to grips with changing societies and a reversal of long-established world views. For those entering the twenty-first century, there is a sense of

---

[25] Cited in Ruth E. Lechte, 'Partnerships for Ecological Wellbeing', *The Ecumenical Review*, Vol. 42, No. 2, April 1990, p. 160.

political, social and economic uncertainty. Christian leaders cannot remain immune to these concerns because churches are part of society, no matter how much they try to be semi-isolationist. If the mainstream churches fail to respond flexibly enough to the major issues facing the new millennium, they are in danger of becoming museum pieces. Oncoming generations will continue to seek a spiritual community, but will reject the mainstream churches if what they offer is too out of step with the reality of the prevailing life situation.

Paul Collins, a liberal Australian former Catholic priest, writer, and reformer, has made the following criticisms of his Church:

> The centralised and absolutist operation of Rome has brought modern Catholicism to a grinding halt. Among the mainstream majority of Catholics in the western world there is a pervasive sense that the church has failed them, that it has not listened to their experience and their needs and that the doctrinal and moral guidance that it offers in many areas is irrelevant... The modern papacy has become the mouthpiece of an increasingly narrow orthodoxy.[26]

---

[26] *The Weekend Australian*, 14-15 February 1998, extracts from Paul Collins, *Papal Power*, Harper Collins Religious. Collins had been under investigation for heresy by the Vatican.

3

Women Seeking Justice

In strongly patriarchal cultures, it is difficult to convince men that a pattern of equal status and mutual agreement would produce a healthier dynamic in relationships. In 'macho' cultures, domination of women appears to be a way of boosting male egos. In his teachings, Jesus stressed humility and respect for others in personal relations. He did not use methods of coercion. Male clerics frequently preach about Jesus' example of servanthood, putting their words into practice on Maundy Thursday by washing the feet of members of their congregation. But, as a general rule, churchwomen are the church members expected to carry out the servile, domestic chores. The continuation of role stereotyping reinforces the outdated assumption that men should play the power and authority roles. This is a social custom which negates Christianity's claim that it is based on love and equity for all people.

Anne Hall, a former Roman Catholic nun, is surprised that the Pope can promote a church based on 'male only power', when the numbers of priests violating women and children are growing daily:

> Power invades all human relations and every relationship can be analysed in terms of its balance of power. The role of the priest in the Catholic Church carries power, and with it ethical responsibilities. It therefore follows that sexual assault in the ministerial relationship is a misuse of power, a betrayal of trust, and a crime.[27]

In July 2010, Pope Benedict XVI surprised Christian women worldwide by declaring that the ordination of a Catholic woman to priesthood was a grave sin against the faith. He made clear that the ordination of a woman would lead to immediate ex-communication and would be considered as serious a crime in Canon Law as child abuse by paedophile male priests. Victim groups immediately protested that criminal offences against children should be given far greater weight than doctrinal arguments over the ordination of women.

The Pope's statement is based on the reasoning, now considered flawed, that Christ only chose male apostles. It ignores the opinion of most Catholic scholars that Mary Magdalene was an apostle, whose role in the early church was downgraded by writers with the agenda of promoting an all-male priesthood. The statement also overlooks the part played by women in the New Testament who founded

---

[27] Anne Hall, 'Religious-Woman Come Forth Dancing', in *Women-Church*, No. 16. Autumn, 1995, p. 38.

and kept alive early Christian communities, including Junia in Rome, whom Paul referred to as an apostle.

Few Christian institutions nowadays have the strong political clout of past ages, but some do retain an internal male power culture, a brotherhood, with customs of secrecy. The present spate of clergy sexual offences across the denominations has exposed how strong this culture of secrecy has been, ensuring a protective shield to safeguard the reputation of the offender. The magnitude of the abuse of children and young adults which has been revealed in the opening years of the Third Millennium has led to a loss of clerical prestige. It has only been in recent years that victims of the abuse have gained the courage to break the silence about their enforced sexual encounters with predatory churchmen.

Women were expected to be particularly discreet when in illicit sexual relationships with clergy, especially those clergy whose church expected them to remain celibate. In her work A Passion for Priests, Clare Jenkins reports on the result of her study of romantic attachments between women and Roman Catholic priests. She found that, while the women involved wanted to be open about their affairs, they were afraid to do so because of what they and the priests stood to lose. Some of the women interviewed had had children fathered by their priestly lovers, two of them had abortions with their partners' consent. There was an acknowledgment that the power which the Church has invested in its priests can act as an aphrodisiac, a mix of the sacred and the sensual, which for women who have been socialised with an ideal of submission, sacrifice and self-denial, can have a sexual attraction.

Bishops and heads of Protestant churches have also been under fire for their failure to handle adequately sexual abuse and adultery committed by employees, both lay and cleric, in church institutions. Neil and Thea Ormerod, in their book When Ministers Sin, considered that 'the misogyny of the early Church Fathers would have provided ample background for patterns of abuse to emerge'. They queried why it has only been in recent times that violent, abusive behaviour is being addressed seriously:

> Here credit must be given to the brave men and women who have dared to break the silence on the issue of incest and sexual abuse in the family. As is well known, when Freud began his investigations in depth psychology, he was shocked by the number of patients who reported sexual abuse in childhood.[28]

This statement confirms that domestic violence and sexual abuse were subjects which customarily were not brought out into the open. While such subjects are now widely discussed and written about in general society today, sexuality is still played down in Christianity, and seldom aired in sermons. Victims of sexual abuse in church situations have found it particularly difficult to penetrate the walls of silence.

The Vatican has been reluctant to address the mounting evidence of sexual abuse by its clergy, made public

---

[28] Neil and Thea Ormerod, *When Ministers Sin: Sexual Abuse in the Churches*, Millennium Books, Alexandria, NSW, 1995, p. viii.

particularly in the United States and Europe. This has been attributed to the Vatican's focus on protecting Roman Catholicism at a time when the Western Church is suffering a dire shortage of priests. When the number of cases of abuse reached epidemic proportions, the Vatican was forced to respond. The Pope apologised to sexual abuse victims, condemning incidences of priestly paedophilia as 'the most grievous form of evil'.

The unmasking of the high incidence of sexual abuse by male priests and the way they have been protected by senior members of the churches has indicated how strong brotherhood links are in the top echelons of Christianity. In her article 'Brotherhoods, Secret Societies and the Patriarchy – What is Never Stated', Lynn Brunet, a lecturer in Art History, points out that secrecy is one of the fundamental principles of brotherhoods. 'The interests of a fellow brother are considered foremost'.[29] Members of fraternities are considered to be 'sacred' and non-members 'profane'. Rituals, such as in Masonic lodges, are a celebration of patriarchy 'in its purest, most primeval form'. The range and influence of fraternities and the strength of their code of silence is clearly mirrored in church hierarchies.

Brotherhood codes have affected how paedophilia is handled in Christian churches. Church hierarchies find it difficult to defrock offending priests, and their protectiveness prevents them from being sufficiently compassionate to victims of abuse. Priests are reluctant to consider that celibacy might give rise to inappropriate sexual behaviour.

---

[29] Lynn Brunet, 'On Brotherhoods, Secret Societies and the Patriarchy - What is Never Stated', in *Women-Church*, No. 30, Autumn, 2002, p. 25.

At the Rome meeting of American cardinals, it was averred that 'a link between celibacy and paedophilia cannot be scientifically maintained'. It was pointed out that married priests in non-Roman Catholic denominations were also guilty of sexual abuse and paedophilia.

According to the late Dr Patricia Brennan, National President of the Movement for the Ordination of Women in Australia and also a specialist clinician concerned with cases of physical abuse of women and children, 'when it comes to moral virtue, the church has set itself up as a specialist institution'. In practice, the church system has failed to protect victims of sexual abuse. Brennan queried:

> What is it about religion and sexual abuse that invites a shocking synergy? Somewhere along the line in church history, sex was given an R rating. It sent the body to a realm where the neurotically forbidden became trammelled in the irresistibly desirable. The Western church made sex its paramount test of self-control, sending generations into self-denial or furtive self-gratification.[30]

The entire area of questions associated with power, patriarchal cultures and sexuality requires much further attention. However, it can be observed that the common existence of patriarchal structures in many churches denies recognition of the historically dominant role played by women in basic faith supporting and faith-transmitting

---

[30] Cited in *Sydney Morning Herald*, 22 February 2002.

activities, especially to following generations. Discounting and downplaying such important roles played by women in the church is likely to be one factor in the absence of younger women in mainstream churches – a decline noted in earlier chapters.

The problem for churchwomen has been, and still is, that despite the amount of spiritual support and voluntary labour they have provided to their churches, their efforts have been largely unrecorded. Church histories reveal that the activities of churchmen, especially clerics and prestigious male laity, overwhelmingly fill the pages, while churchwomen barely rate a mention.

Although the majority of mission workers, at home and abroad, were women, it was men who were appointed to head missionary societies and who received the kudos for mission achievements. Historic records show that Christian leaders indoctrinated women to believe that the Godly path for women to take was to carry out dutifully their allotted tasks, shunning the limelight as much as possible.

Twenty-first century women are much less self-effacing than were their female predecessors. Through working in the public sphere, women have learned that stroking the egos of their male colleagues by playing down their own talents is a dishonest ploy, detrimental for both men and women. Such self-deprecation merely shores up male fantasies about their innate superiority. Continuing to uphold delusions of male superiority within Christian organisations will not attract today's women back to churches.

There have been strong warnings from progressive Christians that mainstream ecclesial systems are approaching obsolescence, and are drastically in need of restructuring. Yet even those leading churchmen of various denominations, who have been supportive of women, have not prioritised the need to eliminate the gender imbalance which permeates every corner of scripture, church teaching and worship. This is understandable, if regrettable. Male-centricity applies especially in monotheistic faiths, from which female divinity has been eliminated and where the One God is portrayed predominantly in male metaphors. Thus, in the 21st century, the oldest Christian denominations remain tied to a patriarchal religious system, which is so geared to ancient male-centric texts and rituals, that to introduce a feminine presence into the corridors of leadership would automatically ring heretical alarm bells.

Gender balancing should not entail replacing patriarchy with matriarchy. Both these systems are based on the principle of the domination of one sex through devaluation of the other. The driving concern in a faith such as Christianity, which claims to value justice and equality, should be to foster the concept of mutual respect and preparedness to share authority. Women are more likely to return to the mainstream of Christianity if the spiritual environment, including perceptions of God, acknowledges that women and men are 'one in Christ', that is of equal value in the sight of God.

There are theologies in existence today, which are more in touch with contemporary people's experiences of God. Many exceptionally progressive religious scholars came to prominence in the second half of the twentieth century, challenging the theological assumptions of the past. Among them were women, including Roman Catholic academics such as Rosemary Radford Ruether, Elizabeth Johnson and

Elisabeth Schüssler Fiorenza. A problem is that the fruits of women's theological and scriptural scholarship have not been promoted by a majority of clergy as essential reading for congregations. Few feminist theological viewpoints have been incorporated into mainstream Christian liturgy and doctrine. So far, Christian leaders – while occasionally acknowledging that the depth of religious scholarship carried out by female scholars has been impressive – have tended to regard their writings as too disquieting for mainstream congregations. Therefore Christianity remains locked into an ethos where the feminine perspective is largely ignored by the majority of those who preach and set down guidelines, i.e. male clerics.

Males have been socialised for millennia to assume leadership roles because of their physical strength and supposedly superior intellect. Where males dominate, particularly in world affairs, there can be a tendency towards condoning war and general aggressiveness. The part religion is playing in activating violence in the opening decade of the 21st century has forced many Christians to acknowledge that the militant, tribal God recorded by the Hebrews in their ancient scriptures, was never a salutary spiritual guide for any society. The continuous portrayal of God as a supporter of 'holy war' is especially dangerous in a world where weapons capable of mass destruction exist.

Christians need to focus on the biblical texts where God is portrayed as a deity, whose priority is love and the wellbeing of all people, irrespective of race, social status or gender.

Undoubtedly, parts of the Bible can be dispiriting for women, despite its many inspirational and beautiful passages. Australian Catholic woman, Popovic, has expressed her exasperation at the way Christian leaders use ancient scriptures to justify the exclusion of women from positions of authority:

> Why does today's society still believe in the Bible? Why are women trying so desperately to find positive images for themselves in those patriarchal stories? Is it the need to validate their existence? Should it not be enough that we *are*? Sadly not in our tradition it seems, because women are still treated as lesser being.[31]

To support her comments, Lany Popovic cites the following passage from Uta Ranke-Heinemann's book *Eunuchs for the Kingdom of Heaven*: 'The whole of Church history adds up to one long arbitrary, narrow-minded, masculine despotism over the female sex... the despotism continues *today*, uninterrupted'. Similarly, Angela West, in her book *Deadly Innocence*, claims that 'if women were guilty of anything, it was of the failure to actualize themselves - the sin of too much self-sacrifice on the altar of the patriarchal gods'.

While a major section of Christianity continues to treat women as the subordinates in its tradition, it leaves itself open to accusations of being unethical. If the Christian faith remains indifferent to issues of sexual discrimination and injustice, then its leaders risk losing their historical status as specialists on moral issues. The ground rules for achieving

---

[31] Lany Popovic, 'Women-Church Future-Church, One Voice', in *Women-Church*, No. 24, April 1999, p. 30.

wholesome societies are increasingly being laid down by social scientists in the secular arena, without reference to religious leaders.

Musimbi Kanyoro, a Kenyan Lutheran, former General Secretary of the World Young Women's Christian Association and member of staff of the World Council of Churches, has commented on the situation for women in church and society:

> At present women are advocating for gender consciousness in the churches and in their societies. Gender refers to the social organization of sexual differences. Culture, religion and science create, reinforce and perpetuate what it means to be man or woman in a particular society. Gender is a primary way of signifying relationships of power. It is one of the several elements used in society to construct relationships in which one person or one group is perceived as superior to the other. Women will continue to challenge ecumenical formation into the next millennium to take gender issues seriously.[32]

A significant event in the approach to the twenty-first century was the celebration of the first half-century of existence of the World Council of Churches (WCC), one of the foremost mainstream Christian ecumenical bodies. An

---

[32] Musimbi Kanyoro, 'A Life of Endless Struggle or Stubborn Hope: An African Feminine Perspective on the Jubilee', *The Ecumenical Review*, Vol. 49, No. 4, October 1997, pp. 408-409.

Assembly was held in Harare, Zimbabwe, in December 1998. At the time of the WCC's inception in 1948, there were strong, well-educated women in the founding committees, urging the new body to take gender issues seriously. As a result, a Women's Desk was established and the concept of men and women in equal partnership in the Church was incorporated into the WCC's ethos. However, it became clear as the years rolled by that equal partnership was in practice not being implemented within the majority of church communities.

To draw greater attention to the inequitable, subordinate situation of many Christian women, in 1988 the WCC launched the Ecumenical Decade of Churches in Solidarity with Women. The aims of the Decade were fourfold: to empower women to challenge oppressive structures in their countries and in the churches; to affirm the decisive contribution of women; to enable churches to free themselves from racism, classism and sexism; and to encourage churches to take actions in solidarity with women.

The Decade of Women was officially closed at the Harare assembly of the WCC in 1998. According to the then General Secretary of the WCC, Dr Konrad Raiser, 'the Ecumenical Decade of the Churches in Solidarity with Women has made a dramatic plea for the space needed to make of the church truly an inclusive community'. He conceded that not all churches supported the WCC's stance on women:

> Many churches today, however, under the pressure of internal and external challenges, are withdrawing behind confessional and institutional lines of defence... Many perceive the World Council of Churches as a functional

agency whose effectiveness is to be evaluated in comparison with the many other specialized international non-government organisations.[33]

Undoubtedly the aims of the Ecumenical Decade of Churches in Solidarity with Women have caused conflicts within the WCC because of the ecclesiological and theological revisions entailed in changing attitudes towards women. One of the problems facing Christian women is that institutionally the WCC's perspective and leadership, despite the principles of gender equality which it has espoused, is still overly male-oriented. This reality results in a lack of priority being accorded to addressing the continuing injustices against women globally. Acknowledgment is made of the extent of violence against women built into cultures as well as the physical abuses they suffer in areas of chronic unrest, but efforts to try to change cultures of violence against women tend to be side-tracked or put into the too-hard basket.

The women working within the WCC are trying to keep women's issues alive. They have considerable access to information concerning the adverse effects on women of gender imbalance. They know the need to maintain a major focus on women through their links with the WCC, since women globally, more than any other human beings, commonly experience impoverishment, injustice and inability to escape from relentless violence.

---

[33] Konrad Raiser, 'Report of the General Secretary to the WCC's Eighth Assembly, Harare, 3-14 December 1998' in *The Ecumenical Review*, Vol. 51, No. 1, January 1999, p. 88.

At a Conference held in Minneapolis in November 1993, to mark the mid-way point in the Women's Decade, it was clear that those women attending were dissatisfied with the progress that had been made in the first five years of the Decade, especially in regard to sexist attitudes. It was recognised that theology built around an exclusively male deity prevented women from benefitting to the full from Christ's liberating gospel. The women who attended the Conference were encouraged not to adhere to androcentric theologies, which deified maleness. Theology had to be rewritten to reflect the ethos of men and women being one in Christ. Such theology would entail an acknowledgement of the divineness of the feminine.

In the weekend before the official opening of the Harare Assembly of the WCC, 1200 women and 30 men came together in what was called 'the Ecumenical Decade of Churches in Solidarity with Women Festival'. This Festival was convened for the specific purpose of both celebrating and analysing the achievements of the Decade. The imbalance of females over males attending the Festival was yet another indication that the Decade had become a women's affair rather than, as had originally been hoped, a concern of all church members, including leaders. There was consensus that its aim to improve the status of women had only partially been achieved, that the churches had not demonstrated that they were solidly behind women. The Decade, in practice, had been much more a Decade of 'Women in Solidarity with Women'. As Beatrice Wood, the chairperson of this Festival, later reported to the Harare

Assembly: 'The Decade has been more than we expected but far less than we dreamed.'[34]

Dr Aruna Gnandason, the co-ordinator of the Decade, spoke of real anxiety among women, who feared that, with the closure of the Decade of Solidarity with Women, the church leaders would merely heave a sigh of relief that they could move on to other business, rather than being constantly reminded of the need to address women's issues.

There was acknowledgement that advances had been made during the Decade in terms of women's ordination and increased laywomen's participation in councils and committees, but these gains were too often offset by discriminatory practices. There was still a tendency in churches to trivialise women's needs, problems and aspirations. Reforming women also had to face the reality that there were churchwomen who were unsupportive of change, thus acting as agents for the maintenance of male supremacy. Churchwomen have been encouraged by church tradition to serve rather than to hold authority, and church tradition tends to be equated with God's will. As a consequence of this, many churchwomen perceive that it is their duty to curb the demands for equal status which their more radical sisters are making.

To ensure that women's issues were not ignored, participants at the Decade of Women Festival drew up a letter addressed to the churches, under the title 'From

---

[34] For a full copy of the 'Letter to the Eighth Assembly of the World Council of Churches from the women and men of the Decade Festival of the Churches in Solidarity with Women' see Trish Madigan, 'Festival, Fetes and Flowers: Women Model New Visions in Harare', *Women-Church*. April 1999, pp 38-41.

Solidarity to Accountability'. This letter was then presented to a plenary session of the Harare Assembly. Its contents focussed on 'the vision of a human community where the participation of each and everyone is valued, where no one is excluded on the basis of race, sex, age, religion or cultural practice, where diversity is celebrated as God's gift to the world.' The women who authored the letter had been united about the inclusion of a statement calling for the elimination of all violence (sexual, religious, psychological, structural, physical, spiritual, and military) and a rejection of the Culture of Violence, with its negative effects on the life and dignity of women. The Harare Assembly was asked to acknowledge that violence against women is a sin. Initiatives put forward as a means of countering the culture of violence included creating opportunities for women to speak out fearlessly, exposing sexual abuse, eliminating all biblical and theological justifications for the use of violence, opposing war and denouncing female genital mutilation, sex-tourism and trafficking of women and children.

The Festival letter also urged Christians to 'declare poverty and all its dehumanising consequences a scandal against God'. Churches were urged to 'unmask the economic forces of death and destruction' and to 'fulfil God's creative intention for accountable stewardship of the earth'. Churches were exhorted to protest 'against all vestiges of colonialism and all forms of neo-colonialism', with a demand for cancellation of the internal and external debts of the world's poorest nations. There was a call for laws to protect women's rights to property and the creation of just economic systems and structures in church and society.

The Festival letter made a special plea to church leaders not to misuse the power and authority which had been delegated to them, pointing out that: 'We, as women, have been and are the victims of this abuse', and 'shall not tolerate its presence any more'. Church leaders were urged to 'encourage more women to take up leadership roles and support them so that they can offer new understandings of and ways of using power'.

The letter also made clear that younger generations wanted structures of domination and oppression replaced by 'new models of organisation, where power is shared and every voice is heard'. The letter envisioned new forms of partnership 'where a leader is someone who helps others to flourish', 'where young and older women work together, and where each is recognised for who they are and what they have to offer'.

For the women seeking change, a major problem has been that the WCC itself has limited powers. The organisation was set up to provide an *open forum* in which representatives of member churches could interact rather than impose any particular viewpoint on a member church. Any suggestion that a particular denomination's rituals, doctrine and practices might contain elements of injustice or lack integrity, could cause offence. Senior clergy are reluctant to admit that a basic religious teaching or practice in their denomination is ethically suspect, fearing this could undermine the status of their church.

Through its Women's Desk, the WCC has provided opportunities for global dialogue on the status of women in the church. But, in top level discussions, WCC officials have been reluctant to draw attention to gender discrimination, especially when interacting with the Roman Catholic and Orthodox churches. This reticence is related to the WCC's Toronto Statement made in 1950. The Toronto Statement declared that the WCC 'deals in a provisional way' and 'does not prejudge the ecclesiological problem'. In other words, the WCC, because it is a forum provider, has 'no ecclesiological position of its own'. Its main role is to be conciliatory and promote unity.

The Toronto Statement creates a paradox, for it restricts the ability of the WCC to be effective as an organisation which seeks to promote justice and integrity. If true to its aims, the WCC would declare boldly that ecclesiology which denies women equality with men in any area of church life is unacceptable ecclesiology because it negates the goals of justice and the integrity of creation.

Conservative Christians contend that issues of sexism and racism are more relevant to the secular than the religious sphere, and thus are a distraction from church order and evangelistic mission. Many church leaders, who are sympathetic to the gender equity problem, are not free to act alone. Even those who have powers to make change, hesitate to use them if such action is going to alienate them from their clergy colleagues and from prestigious laymen.

The WCC has frequently had to tone down ecclesiological criticism in order to maintain dialogue with the hierarchies of the larger denominations, especially those outside the WCC, aware that its image of being more Protestant than Catholic puts it at a disadvantage vis-à-vis the Roman Catholic and Orthodox churches. As Konrad Raiser admits, 'the intensive activity of bilateral dialogues seem to have led to an increased awareness of confessional identity' making the partners in ecumenical dialogue 'more hesitant to engage in a process of learning from one another'.[35]

The decision of the largest Christian denomination, the Roman Catholic Church, not to join the WCC has been a continuing problem in ecumenical dialogue. The WCC gave its support at the 1998 Harare assembly to the creation of a 'Forum of Christian Churches and Ecumenical Organisations' which would include denominations which are not WCC members, such as the Roman Catholic, Pentecostal and Evangelical churches. Opponents of the formation of this new forum have expressed fears that it might create a 'parallel', more conservative ecumenical structure, thus blunting the WCC's cutting edge even further.

Churchwomen are becoming more sensitive to male ploys to sideline women's affairs. It was clear that the women present at the Harare Assembly were determined to increase the female representation on the governing central committee of the WCC. The Orthodox delegates were unhappy with this initiative, reluctant to nominate women representatives to such an important body. There was a noticeable backlash against women among the large Orthodox representation. Vsevlod Chaplin, an official of the Russian Orthodox Church, described the two major issues surfacing at the Assembly, the ordination of women and the use of inclusive language – as 'blasphemy'. But tactics to restrict female representation were not entirely successful. The final vote showed that 39% of the newly elected central

---

[35] Konrad Raiser, 'Report of the General Secretary to the WCC's Eighth Assembly, Harare, 3-14 December 1998' in *The Ecumenical Review*, Vol. 51, No. 1, January 1999, p. 88.

committee would be female, a slight improvement on past percentages, though falling short of the equal gender representation the women present would have preferred.

The frequent response from church officials when criticised for not taking women's issues more seriously, is that 'what has endured for centuries cannot be changed overnight'. This attitude is exemplified in an editorial in the *Church Times* of April 1998 drawing attention to the difficulties the Church of England had experienced in according equal status to women:

> It is unrealistic to expect a culture that has treated women as subordinate to shift quickly, despite the advances made in the past two or three generations.... The exercise of power and authority in the Church generally is far from exemplary, and it is perhaps more accurate to see women priests as simply the latest victims of a discriminatory structure in which too many jobs are not advertised, personal recommendation counts for too much and reputation is more important than ability.[36]

A Church of England survey of women priests carried out in 1998 entitled 'Are Anglican Women Priests Being Bullied and Harassed?', found that 107 of the women priests who responded did report on instances of ill-treatment and discrimination. Rev. Elaine Jones, a vicar in a London parish, was told by a male priest that she should 'be burnt

---

[36] *Church Times*, 24 April 1998.

at the stake' as she was a 'modern-day witch'. Another woman priest was spat upon in the street. The survey's report came to the conclusion that women priests are in a 'uniquely vulnerable position' because ecclesiastical law discriminates against them, and there is no redress to secular legislation because the clergy as a whole are not deemed to be 'employees' in the general understanding of the term.

According to Bishop Richard Holloway, then Primate of the Episcopal (Anglican) Church in Scotland, 'the current debate about women's ordination provides the most pointed contemporary example of the perennial human struggle between moral justice and institutional inertia'.[37] He admitted that Christianity is intrinsically and irredeemably sexist and oppressive to women.

Nevertheless, the entry of women into priesthood has been a step towards gender balance. In the Anglican Communion, 1998 was the year when for the first time women bishops participated in the decennial Lambeth Conference – eleven of them – ending the male exclusivity which has been a feature of this assembly since its inception in 1867. The Lambeth Conference, through its resolutions, establishes guidelines for the Anglican Communion. Although a minority of Anglican bishops deeply resented the presence of the women bishops, the majority accepted them into their fold. Ten years later at the 2008 Lambeth Conference, the numbers of women bishops had swelled, one of whom being the Primate of the Episcopal Church in America, Katharine Jefferts Schori.

---

[37] Richard Holloway (ed.), *Who Needs Feminism?*, SPCK, p. 7.

The pace of women's participation in church affairs at the ordained ministry level has accelerated in many of the Protestant mainstream denominations. Women were first ordained as ministers in the Lutheran Church in 1957 and by 1998 had six women bishops, the Lutheran Church of Australia being one of the few branches which has refused to sanction women's ordination. The first female bishop in the Czechoslovak Hussite Church was installed on 17 April 1999 as Bishop of Olomouc. Presbyterians, Methodists, United and Reform churches in most countries now ordain women to ministry. The Protestant churches that do not ordain women are mainly those which are ultra-conservative and fundamentalist.

As women interact increasingly across confessional borders, progress in one denomination spurs on women's activism in other churches. In July 1996, the first European Women's Synod was held in Gmunden, Austria, at which over 1,000 women from 45 countries and from a range of church affiliations attended. The theme of the Women's Synod was 'Women's Power Changing the 21st Century'. As a member of the executive committee explained: 'the synod wants to confront church, political, economic and cultural leaders with the interests of women on a regional, national and European level'. The Women's Synod set a goal of women's full participation in church decision-making processes, with access to all church ministries, including the Roman Catholic and Orthodox priesthoods. The women declared: 'We give priority to opposing the systematic exclusion of women from positions of authority in church and society'. An international group called Women's

Ordination World-wide (WOW) was launched during the synod.

In November 1999, when Pope John Paul II expressed criticism of women's reform groups, WOW responded with the following Press Release:

> It is completely incompatible with the original Christian principle: 'in Christ there is... no male and female' (Gal 3:28) that the representatives of the Church – and these are only men – use violence and control against the will of Jesus (cf. Luke 22; 25) over women by excluding them from all ordained ministries, merely because of their sex... All the women belonging to WOW will not submit to the Pope's doctrine of the exclusion of women from ordination – for the sake of their human dignity and conscience.[38]

As far as Australian Christian women are concerned, they have to face the reality that Aboriginal women were robbed of considerable religious status and leadership opportunities when they either voluntarily or forcibly became members of patriarchal Christian denominations. Christian institutions in the past supported government policies of taking Aboriginal children away from their mothers and communities, especially if they were of mixed race, often in circumstances where the child's parents had not given consent. White Christians presumed that

---

[38] Cited in *Ordination of Catholic Women News*, Vol. 6, No. 3, December 1999, p. 9.

their cultural values were morally superior to those of the indigenous people, while in practice many Australians who classified themselves as Christians displayed traits of barbarity, exploitation, and lack of compassion towards the indigenous peoples, thus making a mockery of Jesus Christ's gospel of love.

Musimbi Kanyoro has expressed concern about the way the mainly white Northern Hemisphere tends to dominate the South:

> The people of the North need to take Africa seriously. If they are genuinely concerned for Africa, they must first listen to the people of Africa, open their eyes to their needs and stop making funding decisions based on their own ideas and perceptions of Africa.... Church people and other 'Good Samaritans' should be exploring what they can do to change policies and practices of their own societies which contribute to the impoverishment of the African people - unfair compensation for their resources, unfair trade policies, the defilement of their environment and the maintenance in power of leaders who have lost their vision for the good of their own people and consequently lost their people's support.[39]

---

[39] Musimbi Kanyoro, 'A Life of Endless Struggle or Stubborn Hope: An African Feminine Perspective on the Jubilee', *The Ecumenical Review*, Vol. 49, No. 4, October 1997, pp. 408-409.

She added: 'A just society depends on just people. Should that not be the beginning of our motivation to address the jubilee questions?'

Sexism and racism are part of the dualism which pervaded early Christianity, acquired from the philosophies and ideologies in fashion when Christianity was in the process of formation Sexism, racism and classism have been built into the 'immutable moral order' of Christian structures. For many Christian women, and in particular those who are Roman Catholic or Orthodox, the achievement of gender balance is particularly tough because the ground rules can only be changed by male clerical hierarchies. Women, and to a lesser-extent laymen, do not participate in major decision-making and have been deprived of the moral authority to change power imbalances. Because of the institutionalisation of sexism into the Roman Catholic and Orthodox ecclesiastical structures, a mammoth task lies ahead for those female members who have decided to struggle to have their church democratised.

Church leaders have been noticeably reticent about drawing attention to the past and ongoing denigration of women, and this phenomenon can also be discerned in gatherings held under the aegis of the WCC. Outcries against injustice to women should have featured prominently in the conferences and general discussions on 'Ecclesiology and Ethics' which the WCC organised in the closing years of the second millennium. But, from papers which have appeared in various editions of *The Ecumenical Review*, it would appear that the issue of women's Christian right to equal partnership with men in church communities has been played down.

In all fairness to the WCC, one must acknowledge that its creation was a positive initiative, in limited ways a substitute for the major councils of the pre-Reformation period. The WCC has succeeded in bringing together its member churches into a new relationship, less authoritarian than the early Christian Councils. The WCC is to be commended for holding firmly to the opinion that only by dialoguing about major issues of contention can a state of interdenominational tolerance and understanding be achieved. Ecclesiology, the basic belief system of churches, has therefore always been a very important area of discussion for the WCC.

Churches constantly point out the need to strengthen the moral and spiritual fibre of today's society to offset the high levels of corruption and inhumanity which are causing so much death, disease, grinding poverty and social imbalance in the global community. But what if 'God's messengers' are themselves in need of correction?

It is not sufficient to expect relatively powerless churchwomen to do all the chipping away at male hegemonic church ramparts. Those in power need to take remedial action which is commensurate with the Everest-like proportions of the problem. The conservative backlash which has occurred in response to churchwomen's criticisms is one of the basic reasons for the present decline in women's participation in mainstream Western Christianity. As Marie-Eloise Rosenblatt, a Roman Catholic sister, has observed about women in her tradition:

> For some religious women, it becomes impossible to reconcile membership in a religious community with belonging to a

patriarchal church. Fidelity to their spiritual growth as women impels them to reject the ecclesial system which oppresses all women in general and religious women in particular, since numbers of religious communities are so visibly associated canonically with the Church's formal structure and more vulnerable than married and single women to the authoritative directives of a male hierarchy.[40]

Spirituality is ideally a process which frees human beings and enables them to communicate in a more meaningful way with each other and with God. The necessity for change was the driving spirit behind Pope John XXIII's establishment of the Second Vatican Council. This Council has been of great significance in transforming and enlivening Catholicism.

In the official documents issuing from Vatican II, it was stated that 'with respect to the fundamental rights of the person every type of discrimination, whether social or cultural, whether based on sex, race, colour, social condition, language or religion, is to be overcome and eradicated as contrary to God's intent'.[41] Unfortunately, the papal leaders since the Second Council have acted to water down Pope John's anti-discrimination statements.

An example of this dilution process is Pope Paul VI's document *Inter Insigniores* on the exclusion of women from

---

[40] Marie-Eloise Rosenblatt, 'We Changed our Minds: The Effect of Feminist Spirituality on Women's Religious Life and Men in the Church', CCVI Communiqué, Vol. 7, No. 3, p. 28.

[41] Second Vatican Council, Pastoral Constitution *Gaudium et Spes*, 29 (7 December 1961), Acta Apostolicae Sedis 58 (1966), pp. 1048-9.

ordained ministry, issued in 1976. Clearly *Inter Insigniores* was formulated to inform those calling for the elimination of sexual discrimination at all levels that this basic right did not apply to the ordained priesthood. This decision ran contrary to the findings of the Pontifical Bible Commission, which in April 1975 noted unanimously that the New Testament made no statement that women could not be priests. A majority (12-5) of the Bible Commission declared that Christ's will would not be violated if women were ordained.

In the Gospels, there is no definitive statement that apostles had to resemble Jesus' gender. The 'Twelve Apostles' came to symbolise the continuity of Jesus' new movement with the twelve tribes of Israel. The ministry carried out in the early churches was not restricted to the 'Twelve' but was open to other apostles and disciples, and it is clear that Paul had many female co-workers.

If, as the Roman Catholics and Orthodox churches claim, the priest represents the Church *in persona Christi*, then women as well as men can be priests. Christ's humanness – not his gender – is essential to his role as mediator. Were it not so, one could argue that half the human race, i.e. women, are unredeemed. Nor does Jesus' maleness affect the substance of the Incarnation, which must be seen as God assuming the whole of our human nature with its twofold sexual expression.

Certainly patriarchal traditions existed in the Roman colonial society in which Jesus carried out his ministry, but New Testament accounts indicate time and time again that Jesus was prepared to break male dominant conventions in his interaction with women. Jesus did not exclude women from his movement. He encouraged them to play active roles, such as the assignment to the Samaritan woman at the well to proclaim his messiahship within her community. Jesus appeared first to Mary Magdalene after his resurrection and her selection as the one to tell 'the others' indicates that Jesus considered her to be a senior person in his movement, especially after so many of the male apostles deserted him during his trial and crucifixion. Mary Magdalene is often referred to as 'the apostle to the apostles'. The New Testament and other literature of the period indicate that women played important leadership roles in the early church, for example, Phoebe, Lydia and Junia.

Any institution, and especially an ecclesial institution professing to emulate Jesus Christ's gospel of love and justice for all peoples, can only be regarded as flawed if it advocates that one gender is intrinsically superior to the other. Rule by a dominant privileged group results in the excluded group being forced to accept the ideals and values of the dominator. This is a similar structure to the colonialism which has left two-thirds of the population of the world at the end of the second millennium living in a situation of appalling poverty. In the secular world, colonialism represented the hegemony of one nation over another. Ecclesial colonialism is the hegemony of churchmen over churchwomen.

Many Christians today believe that mutuality and shared responsibility should form the moral basis of governance and ordering. This is the basis of the Christian principle of a community being 'a royal priesthood of all believers'. Such a principle is decentralised and democratic, with equal opportunity for all. When gender serves as an ideology for male dominance and female subservice, then the institution has a built-in destructive, anti-Christian force.

It is the anti-Christian force of maintaining tradition and not admitting past ecclesial errors which lies at the root of institutionalised Christianity's decline today.

4

The Devaluation of Christian Women

Christianity claims to be based on the teachings and example of Jesus Christ. Jesus challenged and critiqued the religious and socio-political structures in his society. At the time of his earthly mission, Palestine was under Roman colonial rule, the people suffering extreme deprivation through over-taxation and arbitrary confiscation of land and property. The Jewish religious hierarchy was forced to collaborate with the Romans in return for non-interference in Jewish worship.

The Kingdom of God, which Jesus proclaimed, ran counter to the prevailing Roman imperial culture. The ethos of the Jesus Movement was to focus on love and concern for all people, including enemies. Jesus prioritised ministry to the underprivileged, social outcasts, the powerless and those with debilitating health problems. Wealth-sharing rather than wealth accumulation was expected of Jesus' followers. In his movement, the structures were flexible rather than rigid or hierarchical. Women were treated as valued members of the group.

Jesus moved away from traditional work and family obligations. For him, these were of lesser importance than mission and outreach. Jesus' call to discipleship required of his followers a willingness to forsake all, including the customary duties required in a Jewish family. This was a dramatic cultural reversal for the women in his group, because their roles in Jewish culture and tradition were centred on serving their husband and family within domestic confines. The presence of women in the Jesus Movement indicates that there were independent Jewish and Gentile women who had such strong faith in Jesus that they were prepared to risk the consequences of following him.

Women came to the fore in keeping the momentum of Jesus' mission alive in the period following his crucifixion. Professor Susanne Heine, in her work *Women and Early Christianity*, points out that 'the special significance of women for the spread of Christian faith in the first century and beyond has been stressed in many exegetical works since the beginning of our 20th century'. Heine observes that Paul personally did not found all the communities he visited:

> Many women whom he mentions as his fellow workers had not become Christians as a result of him. When Paul appeared, there was already a series of communities, like that in Rome, and Paul met women of acknowledged status

who were actively engaged in building up the community independently of him.[42]

In the Acts of the Apostles and in Paul's writings, both frequently refer to women in positions of responsibility in nascent Christian communities. There was Phoebe, the deacon of the community in Cenchrae, the eastern harbour of Corinth. Further afield, there was Junia in Rome, who, with her husband Andronicus, was described as being pre-eminent among the apostles. Women such as Lydia at Philippi and Mary, the mother of John Mark in Jerusalem, were in charge of house churches.

Admittedly, Jesus' lack of discrimination against women is a minor theme in the Gospels, but that it existed is indisputable. Jesus' egalitarian attitude has not been highlighted in sermons and scholarly works in the years following his death, mainly because most clergy, biblical scholars and theologians have viewed women from prevailing patriarchal perspectives. The focus in New Testament studies has for centuries been on the actions and writings of male persons. However, Lesley Massey sees liberation of women from male domination as an underlying theme in the New Testament.[43] Jesus Christ's support for an attitude of servanthood in human relationships has been misinterpreted to imply that subservience is the sanctified role for women. But when Jesus, as a male human being,

---

[42] Susanne Heine, *Women and Early Christianity*, SCM Press, London, 1987, p. 86.
[43] Lesley F. Massey, *Women and the New Testament – An analysis of Scripture in the light of New Testament Era Culture*. McFarland and Company Inc., North Carolina, USA.

demonstrated the servant role required of his followers by washing his disciples' feet, he showed that such acts of service to others applied to men as well as women.

Christianity had been brought to Rome by pilgrims from the East or by Christians connected with the Roman administration. Early Christianity in Rome consisted of a system of autonomous house churches. These small communities attracted many women, and there is evidence both in scripture and other writings of the time that women played leadership roles in them.

In terms of Gentile members of the early churches, it is possible that some of the women already had experience in leading religious ceremonies. While men dominated politics and economic life, women were permitted to lead private religious rites, although when families worshipped together, the husband took priority over his wife. The most important priest of the highly regarded goddess Athena was a woman, who held her position for life. Women also played prophetic roles, especially at Delphi, where they were believed to be the mouthpieces of gods and goddesses. Greek and Roman men had their own religious cults, from which women were excluded.

The phenomenon of women playing important roles in early formative periods of religious movements has occurred in most of the major faiths. In Buddhism and Islam, for example, attempts had been made initially to improve the situation of women, but the subsequent development of traditions and interpretations of scriptures and theology tended to become increasingly male-dominant, with unfavourable attitudes towards female office-bearers. As Professor Wesley Ariarajah comments in his book *Not*

Without my Neighbour, 'most traditions pushed women back into a subordinate position, fixed their roles in the family and society, barred them from interpreting scriptures and denied them the kind of leadership that would bring about real change'.[44]

Ariarajah's comments certainly applied to the developing Christian faith. Increasingly, women were restricted to inferior roles, especially when the rituals of worship became elaborate and priestly. By the sixth century, when Christianity was closely tied to secular rule, women in leadership positions, such as deacons and presbyters, had almost been phased out. From then on, women's religious leadership operated mostly from within the walls of convents. Abbesses did exercise considerable influence in church circles generally until the thirteenth century, when their economic and power bases were undermined.

A major factor used to justify the removal of women from church leadership was the constant denigration of their religious worth by early Church Fathers. These theologians were so closely attuned to Greek and Roman perspectives, in which masculinity was adulated to divine heights, that they lost sight of Jesus' egalitarian and non-hierarchical values. As a result, Christian philosophy, ecclesiology, moral ethics and theology were formulated and institutionalised predominantly by churchmen imbued with negative attitudes towards women. When Christian theology – the study of the attributes of God and God's relationship with the world and its inhabitants – was genderised to

---

[44] S. Wesley Ariarajah, *Not Without My Neighbour: Issues in Interfaith Relations*, Risk Books, WCC Publications, Geneva, 1999, p. 64.

assume that Deity was *wholly masculine*, the after-effect was the institutionalisation of a jaundiced religious view of womanhood.

American theologian Elizabeth Johnson points out that emphasis on the model of the male-only divine is deeply rooted in the ideal of ruling men within a solid patriarchal structure.[45] Johnson contrasts the prevailing situation with one of gender balance, pointing out that, if mutuality is viewed as moral excellence, then holy mystery is free and interactive rather than distant, reigning and requiring obedient submission.

Ted Lambert, a former Roman Catholic priest, who was obliged to forsake his official priestly duties when he decided to marry, has described how negative the religious impact of patriarchal religion has been on women:

> Injustice to women is institutionalised. It is in the system. What system? The patriarchal system of close to 5000 years, under which the legal frameworks were manmade, the family was structured around property rights, the entire Bible was written by men, and culture has been case hardened in it. The task of reform seems impossible. But nothing is impossible with God. There is no doubt where Christians should start. We have im-bibled this venomous milk. We must depatriarchise the Bible. Like ergot in milk, we have a terrible taste of male in our Revelation...

---

[45] E. A. Johnson, *She Who Is: The Mystery of God in Feminist Theological Discourse*, Crossroad, New York, 1995, p. 69.

> Clerics believe that God (forgive the blasphemy) gives males his (sic) power. But God is not Supermale, reserving his power to his sons. God is love. Therein lies the only just power, the power of love.[46]

A biological supposition used to bolster patriarchal traditions in the early church was related to the Greek philosopher Aristotle's theory that only men were progenitors. Aristotle believed that there was one sex, but two forms, male and female. According to Aristotle, semen was cast into the womb as seed into the earth. Embryonic development was activated by the semen and nourished by the mother's blood. Male foetuses ensued if the seed were given sufficient heat and vital spirit in the uterus. Females resulted from insufficient heat and passion being attained in the womb. Thus women were 'failed males', only fit for lesser, servile roles.

The incorrect biological construct that women lacked ova constituted a major factor in reducing women's former high status as the main child producer and nurturer, on whom the tribe depended for new life and growth. When it was assumed that only male semen produced the child, it was possible to argue that a woman was merely a provider of a site for foetal growth, just as the earth provided nourishment for plant seed. Further suppositions were formulated aimed at undermining the value of women, such as statements that females were basically vacuous creatures, while males had

---

[46] T. Lambert, 'The Organ Stop Named Woman' in *Cross-Reference*, Journal of the Epiphany Association (Queensland) Inc., Vol. 2, No. 1, May 1995, p. 15.

higher intellects, which allowed their souls to transcend their earthly trappings. So, ontologically, moral philosophers and theologians proclaimed that women were both physically and morally inferior human beings. As Kim Power points out in her work on Augustine, the medical discovery that women had ovaries and therefore contributed seed to the procreation process, triggered off the women's movement in the nineteenth century.[47]

Influential male church leaders and moral philosophers in the first five centuries following Jesus' earthly ministry contributed significantly to the discrediting of female Christians. Quality of Christian devotion became associated with freedom from sexual involvement with a female body. Sensuality was abhorred. Sexual intimacy was condemned as a negative side effect of the Fall rather than being regarded as a natural part of God's creation plan. Celibacy and virginity were high among Christian virtues. Marriage had to be permitted to ensure the continuation of the human race but was considered to be 'holy' only if intercourse were restricted to the production of children.

Male Christian leaders and theologians were clearly heavily influenced not only by Aristotle but also by the negative attitudes towards women held by learned men in the societies in which they lived and worked. Early theologians were also influenced by Platonism, in which sacred love was associated with the soul and earthly love associated with the body. The Hellenistic Jewish thinker Philo of Alexandria, categorised women as 'weak, easily

---

[47] Kim Power, *Veiled Desire: Augustine's Writing on Women*, Darton Longman and Todd, London, 1995, p. 9.

deceived, the cause of sin, lifeless, diseased, enslaved, sluggish'.[48] There was a tendency to attribute to women the qualities of the fertility Goddess, the Earth Mother, characterised by passion, lust and fleshliness. Earth was seen as the arena of sexuality, procreation and death. Transcendence was achieved by freeing oneself from earthly things, including the female body. Rosemary Ruether points out that in Greek mythology, the most dignified female figures were virgin, and this concept was transferred to Jesus' mother. Sexuality and maternity were considered to be inferior powers and this was reflected in Greek society where wives had scant legal or political status.

In the early Church, sustained attacks on the female nature not surprisingly led to doubts being raised as to whether women were fully human and whether they possessed souls. The latter assumption was no doubt related to Plato's specious argument that women came about through a physical degeneration of the human being. According to Plato, 'it is only males who are created directly by the gods and are given souls'.[49] Moral philosophies, which for centuries were framed by clerical males, tended to overemphasise the faults in women, while at the same time being lenient towards male inadequacies and misdemeanours. Yet Church history records that church leaders, including popes and bishops, were often morally lax and corrupt.

Woman today are so knowledgeable about the functions of the human body that they do not realise the close

---

[48] Cited on Women Priests' Website – www.womenpriests.org.
[49] Cited on Women Priests' Website - www.womenpriests.org.

correlation between women's inferior status in Christianity and the assumption over almost two thousand years that the female merely contributed nourishment to the formation of the child in the womb. The mistaken belief that males were the main progenitors provided a powerful rationale for patriarchy. Patriarchy is a social structure which derives from two Greek terms, patros (father) and arche (ruling power/authority), in which males are viewed as eligible to reach the apex of power, but in which females and children are always subordinate. Elizabeth Johnson believes that 'religious patriarchy is one of the strongest forms of this structure, for it understands itself to be divinely established'.[50]

In the dualistic worldview, which has influenced so much of Christianity, God is equated with perfection and sanctity and the Devil with sin and evil. When Godhead, in its Trinitarian form, was canonised as male (although the Spirit as God's Wisdom had in the Hebrew scriptures been anthropomorphised as female), it was not surprising that women would conversely be associated with evil and human frailty. But, as Nel Noddings points out in her work *Women and Evil*, if females are depicted as evil, when they are acknowledged also to be created in the image of God, then it is the depicters – the developers of theologies which contain male-biased mythologies – who are the wrongdoers.[51]

---

[50] E. A. Johnson, *She Who is: The Mystery of God in Feminist Theological Discourse*, Crossroad, New York, 1995, p. 23.

[51] See Nel Noddings, *Women and Evil*, University of California Press, Berkeley, 1989, pp. 2-3.

A strong bias against women was clearly evident in the very influential writings of Augustine of Hippo at the beginning of the fifth century. According to Augustine, the patriarchal order was simply 'peace', the only alternative to social chaos.[52] Augustine also asserted: 'Nor can it be doubted, that it is more consonant with the order of nature that men should bear rule over women, than women over men.'[53] Women, because they aroused male passions, were condemned as naturally carnal, corruptive creatures.

If it is assumed that only the male is theomorphic, women are reduced to being ontological, biological and sociological dependants. As Kari Borrisen points out in her article 'Male/Female Typology in the Church', this inequality is exemplified in I Corinthians 11:7 – 'man [the male] ... is the image and glory of God, but woman is the glory of man'. The soul's higher functions were symbolised as male and the lower functions as female. Borrisen draws attention to the arguments to support this view put forward by Augustine:

> In the *De Trinitate*, Augustine takes the man/woman bodily differentiation as a symbol of the soul's higher/lower functions. Higher reason (typified in the male) contemplates eternal verities; lower reason (typified by the female) provides for temporal needs. This

---

[52] Cited in Margaret R. Myles, *Carnal Knowing*, p. 23.
[53] Augustine, *On Concupiscence*, Book I, Chapter 10.

exegesis supposes a hierarchy of the sexes and a rigid distribution of male and female roles.[54]

Augustine's interpretation also suggests that a woman's femininity is not in God's image, only masculinity is in God's image. Woman's humanity is theomorphic but not her femininity. So, unlike the male, there is a break between a woman's humanness and her sex. Augustine could concede no femininity in God because woman represents the *ratio inferior*.

James Nelson, writing on Christian ethics, is of the opinion that when legal structure took precedence over nature, women lost their biological prestige:

> This struggle to break with the earlier biological consciousness led men to project that very consciousness upon women. It was women now, who were the biological beings from whom men must be separated and in relation to whom men must be superior. Thus a series of ritual taboos arose which marked women, particularly through menstruation and childbirth, as 'unclean'.[55]

The label of 'uncleanliness' has always been a strong negative force in belief systems which focus on 'purity' as an ideal. The demonisation of women's special biological

---

[54] K. Borresan, 'Male/Female Typology in the Church', Theological Digest, 31:1, (Spring, 1984), p. 23.
[55] James B. Nelson, *Embodiment: An Approach to Sexuality and Christian Theology*, SPCK, London, 1979, p. 61.

functions underlay much of the moral theology established by Christian patriarchs and still exists in the major Christian denominations, despite advances in knowledge about how bodies function. Revised moral theologies which free the natural female flows from impurity assumptions are an urgent reform needed in the new millennium. The moral basis of a 'pure' ethic needs to emphasise justice, love and equality of the sexes. Biological difference should not be a tool to maintain male dominance.

Dualism, in conjunction with flawed biological determinism, has provided justification for patriarchal Christian systems. The deep structural bias against women, which developed in Early Christianity, resulted in the female-affirming Jesus movement being restructured to conform to the male-dominant systems – Graeco-Roman, pagan, Jewish and political – in existence in the Mediterranean region and throughout the Roman Empire. The rituals which the Church developed had much in common with Jewish temple culture, which was female-exclusive.

The Gnostic writings, though often viewed as liberating for women, also contained examples of prevailing gender assumptions. The concluding logion (114) of the Coptic Gospel of Thomas, believed to be on the periphery of Christian Gnosticism, states that, if Mary is to realise salvation, she must become male.

> Jesus said, 'Behold, I myself shall guide her so
> as to make her male, that she too may become
> a living spirit like you men. For every woman

who makes herself male will enter the kingdom of heaven'.[56]

There is some speculation that this verse was not included in the original document. Marvin Meyer, in his paper on the male and female categories in the Gospel of Thomas, comments that there is scholarly opinion that logion 114 might represent a later addition, appended by Christian monks.[57]

The Protestant Reformation, which surfaced in the twelfth century and peaked in the sixteenth, was successful in freeing regions of the Christian church from tight centralised control. One negative effect was that the Reformers reduced the power which celibate women had exercised within religious orders, placing renewed emphasis on marriage and motherhood as women's most important roles as Christians. Male headship and authority had by now become an entrenched tradition, regardless of the fact that it was grounded in secular philosophies which ran contrary to the Christian ideal of gender equality proclaimed in Galatians 3:28. While acknowledging the Virgin Mary's importance as the mother of Jesus, the Protestant' Reformers rejected her as a supernatural figure to be adored or used as an intercessor.

---

[56] Cited in Marvin W. Meyer, 'Making Mary Male: The Categories 'Male' and 'Female' in the Gospel of Thomas', *New Testament Studies*, Vol. 31, 1985, p.561. This Coptic work, discovered in 1945, is one of the tractates in the Nag Hammadi Library. It is believed that the Mary referred to is most likely to be Mary Magdalene.

[57] *Ibid.*

The Protestant emphasis on 'the Word' contained in the Bible, which was available in regional languages in Reformation times, again worked in favour of male human beings. God was visualised and proclaimed as a Supreme Patriarch, stern and authoritarian, with scant attention to those verses in scripture where God is depicted as a mother who loved and nurtured all creation. The Reformers continued to view the female body in a disparaging way, but now justification for this view was linked with Scripture. The frailty of women was equated with Eve the seducer, or Mary Magdalene the whore, both undeserved epithets. As John Calvin declared: 'Let man exercise authority with moderation, let woman be satisfied with the state of subjection and not take it amiss that she is made inferior to the more distinguished sex'.[58]

Because the male perspective was accepted as the norm, the majority of Christians, including females, failed to recognise how flawed were the writings on women by revered church scholars and Church Fathers. This problem has persisted into the 21st century, although with increasing criticism by the rising body of female theologians. For example, when writing on 'Calvin and Human Rights', J. M. Vorster, director of the School of Ecclesiastical Studies at Potchefstroom University for Christian Higher Education, points out that, in his prolific writings, Calvin stressed that all people are equal before God and are equal before the law.[59] Vorster observes that 'liberty' was an important

---

[58] Cited in Warren Farrell, *The Liberated Man*, Bantam, New York, 1975, p. 158.
[59] J. M. Vorster, 'Calvin and Human Rights', in *The Ecumenical Review*, Vol. 51, No. 2, April 1999, pp. 214 and 217.

principle in Calvin's theology. 'In the religious sphere, he emphasised the liberty of the believer in Christ and the fact that a believer can be bound only by total obedience to God.' Despite this commendation of Calvin's principles of equality and liberty, Vorster completely fails to perceive Calvin's lack of recognition that women – i.e. half the human race – were not equal before the law nor did they have equal status in institutionalised Christianity.

Similarly, in the work of French religious sociologist, Professor Dominique Colas, *Civil Society and Fanaticism*, the author provides a detailed account of the philosophical, theological and political thought worlds of Luther, and other Reformers.[60] What is evident is how completely the female perspective was ignored in the writings of these men, their main concern being to close convents and make sure that women were safely locked into marriage and domesticity.

Luther, in his *Lectures on Genesis*, clearly attributes woman's inferiority to Eve's fall from grace, declaring that 'if the woman had not been deceived by the serpent she could have been the equal of Adam in all respects'.[61] Luther ignores the fact that Jesus, often called the 'New Adam', had an opposite perspective on women's status. Thus Luther gave more weight to a Jewish creation myth than to Gospel reality.

Luther admitted that women's confinement to the home, childbearing and rearing was not an unmixed blessing. It

---

[60] D. Colas, *Civil Society and Fanaticism: Conjoined Histories*, Translated by Amy Jacobs, Stanford University Press. 1978.

[61] Cited in Margaret R. Miles, *Carnal Knowing: Female Nakedness and Religious Meaning in the Christian West*, Vintage Books, New York, 1991, p, 107.

was a blessing with strong components of punishment for Eve's misdemeanour. Luther was lenient to Adam, claiming that he was not deceived by the serpent, 'he was deceived by his wife', and ate the fruit out of love for her. Because Eve sinned, women must for ever be subordinate to men:

> The rule remains with the husband, and the wife is compelled to obey him by God's command. He rules the house and the state, wages war, and defends his possessions... The woman, on the other hand, is like a nail driven to the wall...She sits at home...deprived of the ability of administering those affairs that are outside and that concern the state.[62]

What becomes evident is that Christian explanations of male dominance and female subordination were influential in bestowing moral respectability to societies and institutions which were governed by men. As Margaret Miles comments in her work *Carnal Knowing*, 'gender hierarchy was established as normative and inevitable for human beings'.[63] Women, because they were marginalised in public life, were particularly vulnerable. They lived in constant danger of misrepresentation and had few powers to defend themselves, as was witnessed during the various witch hunts which occurred in Europe and America from the fifteenth to eighteenth centuries.

---

[62] *Ibid.*, p. 112, citing from *Lectures*.
[63] *Ibid.*

The English theologian, Gillian Paterson, points out that Christian tradition has consistently underplayed the role of women in the gospel stories, observing:

> Take, for example, the extraordinary liberties it has taken with the character of Mary Magdalene. I grew up with an image of her as a reformed prostitute, sexually enticing and perhaps a bit mad, whom Jesus, out of his (sometimes misplaced) generosity, had befriended. What seems to have happened is that tradition amalgamated a number of gospel women, and presented them to the faithful as one person. I have heard it stated from the pulpit that Mary Magdalene was the sinful woman who poured ointment over Jesus' head, the woman taken in adultery who escaped stoning only because of Jesus' intervention and maybe even Mary of Bethany.[64]

Most Biblical scholars are agreed today that there is no evidence that Mary Magdalene was an immoral woman. In Luke's Gospel (8:2) she is named as a person from whom Jesus cast out seven demons, but evil spirits were usually associated with illness or mental problems. Paterson is of the opinion that 'Mary was likely to have been a leading member of a group of respectable women, some of them relatively affluent, who assisted Jesus in his ministry'.[65]

---

[64] Gillian Paterson, *Still Flowing: Women, God and Church*, Risk Books, WCC Publications, Geneva, 1999, p. 25.
[65] *Ibid.*, p. 26.

Feminist theologians believe that in Christian tradition the significance of Mary Magdalene and the other women at the tomb on the first Easter Day was deliberately played down because it might suggest that women should be allowed to share in church leadership. Although Jesus exhorted his disciples to remember the woman at Bethany who anointed him for burial with precious ointment, very little attention has been paid to the woman's action or her sensitivity to Jesus' coming ordeal on the Cross. (Matthew 26:6-13) As Paterson points out, 'Christian tradition has been entirely unable to deal with the implications of a strong, competent woman, loved and trusted by Jesus, and holding a leadership role among his friends. It was crucial for those who were responsible for the early church that the principle of male leadership – the apostolic succession itself – should be given the imprimatur of history.'[66]

Rosemary Ruether, has identified three psychic layers developing in sexual history: firstly the servant role of women, secondly the evilness of women's bodies, and thirdly, the spiritualised ideal woman, mother and virgin. The pure mother became the guardian of religion and morality in the private sphere of home and in the domestic roles reserved for women in the Church.[67] Virgin Mary, the mother of Jesus, was regarded as the epitome of perfect womanhood. When Christianity was endorsed as the religion of the Roman Empire, the Virgin Mary became a

---

[66] *Ibid.*
[67] See Rosemary Radford Ruether, *New Woman, New Earth*, Dove, Melbourne, 1975, Chapter 1.

substitute for the much-loved Mother Goddess figures, such as Isis and Artemis.

Especially in the Roman Catholic Church, the Virgin Mary became a cultic figure. Expanding doctrines about her nature tended to represent a male view of what constituted an acceptable Christian female icon. Decrees were issued which claimed that her impregnation by God did not involve the usual sexual intercourse between men and women, nor was her hymen broken, even following the birth of Jesus. Her mother, Anna, was also said to have been free of sin when giving birth to Mary. That Mary gave birth to any further children was denied, despite the scriptural evidence that Jesus had siblings.

Mary as the serene, eternally youthful mother, cradling her child Jesus, was the aspect which probably endeared her most to Christians, both male and female. Although not included in the Trinity, she was considered to be the 'Queen of Heaven'. By the Middle Ages, the stature of the Virgin Mary was rising beyond her motherhood role. In his article 'The Priesthood of Mary', published in the English Catholic journal, The Tablet, in 1999, John Wijngaards points out that most Catholics today are unaware of the historically important link between Mary and the priesthood. According to Wijngaards, 'the priestly role ascribed to Mary went well beyond the common priesthood of the faithful'. Wijngaards took as an example the words of a Jesuit, Ferdinand Chirino de Salazar (1576-1646) who wrote: 'Christ, "the anointed", poured out the abundance of his anointing on Mary, making her a saint, a queen and a priest forever. Mary obtained a priesthood more eminent and excelling than that possessed by anyone else'.[68]

There exist several paintings and mosaics depicting Mary dressed in priestly vestments. Examples of these are a painting of the Annunciation from Gengenbach, Germany, dated ca. 1150, and a fifteenth century painting entitled 'Le sacerdoce de la Vierge' from Amiens in France. In this painting Mary, dressed in a priest's chasuble and stole, is standing at the altar distributing Holy Communion. The Pope is on his knees before her.

The tradition of Mary the Priest was maintained until the end of the nineteenth century. Pope Pius, writing in 1873, supported the tradition by declaring that 'from his virginal conception to his cruel death, Mary united herself so closely to the sacrifice of her divine Son that she has been called the 'Virgin Priest' by the Fathers of the Church'.[69]

Thus there is evidence of an enduring and important recognition of the priestly role of Mary in the Roman Catholic church. Wijngaards points out that Catholic scholars were aware that, when acclaiming Mary as a priest, there was a gender complexity in the statement. Women, as 'incomplete human beings', could not be ordained to priesthood. Also their monthly periods made them ritually impure. Mary had to be perceived as a woman who was somehow biologically different from other women to qualify for priesthood.

---

[68] John Wijngaards, 'The Priesthood of Mary', in *The Tablet*, Vol. 253, 4 December 1999, pp. 1638-40.
[69] *Ibid.*

Belief in and discussion about Mary's priesthood came to an abrupt end in the early twentieth century when the Vatican forbade the practice of portraying Mary as a priest. In 1926, it was declared that devotion to Mary Priest 'is not approved and may not be promoted'. Wijngaards poses the question: 'Is it a coincidence that just at that time the campaign for women's ordination began to stir in other Christian churches?' The ban was successful. By the end of the twentieth century, few Roman Catholic lay people were aware that Mary had ever been extolled for her priesthood.

The priestly tradition of Mary was not venerated in the Orthodox churches. Australian theologian, Leonie Liveris. has commented that one of the main reasons given for the rejection of women priests is that 'women cannot be ordained because the Virgin Mary, the Theotokos [God Bearer], was never called to exercise a sacramental priestly function'.[70] This is confirmed in a statement by Pope Shenouda III of the Coptic Orthodox Patriarchate:

> If women were called to priesthood, the first woman priest in the world would have been the Virgin Mary. No woman in the world is more holy than Saint Mary... And Saint Mary the Virgin did not claim to be a priest. She was the spiritual mother of all the Apostles, but she did not claim to be a priest.[71]

---

[70] Leonie Liveris, 'Time to Speak of Feminism in the Orthodox Church', in M. Confey, D. A. Lee and J. Nowotny (eds.), *Freedom from Entrapment: Women Thinking Theology*, Dove, North Blackburn, 1995, p. 198.

[71] Pope Shenouda III, *Ordination of Women and Homosexuality*, Coptic Orthodox Publishers Association, London, 1993, p. 41.

We see that Orthodox tradition, like that of other sections of Christianity, considered motherhood to be the highest calling for women. But motherhood *per se* does not automatically grant women status in the Church. Married women are usually assigned domestic roles in congregations. As Liveris explains the situation, 'always women carry with them the past reputation of Eve, always they travel towards the sinless and unobtainable, but beloved, Mary the Mother of God'.

Many Christian women recall that they were allowed more leadership. opportunities in the church as young single women. On marrying, they experienced a loss of esteem because the 'male headship' doctrine appeared to be particularly applicable to married women. Yet, if women requested lay positions more in keeping with their non-domestic talents, especially if they were professionals, they tended to be branded as 'agitators', told they were acting in an un-Godly fashion.

Historical analysis has revealed that in most church systems there has been an underlying premise that males have a divine mandate to be the rulers of the Church. This premise is still discernible in most mainstream Christian denominations, though more strongly espoused in Roman Catholicism and the Orthodox churches. While the male/female imbalance is slowly changing in the Anglican Communion and the Protestant churches through women's acceptance into ordained ministry, patriarchal views persist. For example, the late Dr Kenneth Cable, a well-known Australian historian, remarked several years ago at an Anglican history seminar, 'The last thing we want is the feminisation of the Church!'[72] But, in terms of membership numbers, the Australian Anglican Church is already feminised. Statistics show that the proportion of Australian Anglican female adherents in the twentieth century was consistently two-thirds of total membership.[73]

Resistance to women having religious authority is noticeable today in the burgeoning Pentecostal churches, an indication that the sexist attitudes prevailing in the first millennium will be extraordinarily difficult to eradicate. Structural reformation will require a drastic re-evaluation of the accepted norms in theology, ecclesiology and moral philosophy, especially in regard to biological determinism. Women's bodies and souls must be seen to be as holy as those of men. Evil must be stripped of its association with the feminine.

Feminist and liberation theologies are now increasingly taught in Protestant and Roman Catholic seminaries, both having roots in struggles against oppression. Although not the only antidote for entrenched patriarchy, these theologies at least introduce fresh perspectives which expose the weaknesses in the old system. As women constitute the majority of poor and oppressed people in the world, the Church needs to stress as strongly as possible, in words and practice, the dignity of the female sex.

---

[72] Australian Anglican History Seminar, 27-28 September 1997, New College, University of New South Wales, Sydney.
[73] For confirmation of this percentage, see D. Hilliard, 'The Ties that Used to Bind', p. 7. Paper presented at Australian Anglican History Seminar, 27-28 September. 1997.

It may be difficult for male clerics to make the leap into gender equity. No group likes to surrender its privileged position. In the case of Roman Catholicism this is particularly pertinent, for the Vatican, ruled by a celibate male hierarchy, enjoys nation status. To start to introduce gender equity and democracy into the Vatican state, ordained women and lay men and women must be allowed to participate in its central decision-making processes. This is why the ordination of women is an essential stage in any reformation processes.

So far, the Vatican is determinedly resisting any attempts to undermine its clerical male power base. Even the close proximity of women priests from other denominations invokes resentment. When on 3 November 1996, Ruth Cecilia Monge Teresa de Erazo was ordained as an Anglican priest in Rome's St Paul's Within-the-Walls, a senior Vatican theologian, Monsignor Rino Fisichella, declared that she was an 'apostate' and not a real priest. He particularly resented a woman priest, even though Anglican, being situated within the See of Rome.[74]

Dr Lavinia Byrne, a member of the Institute of the Blessed Virgin Mary, has been forced to leave her religious community because the Vatican did not approve of the publication in 1998 of her book *Woman at the Altar*. The book was condemned by the Congregation of the Doctrine of Faith, headed then by Cardinal Joseph Ratzinger, who is now Pope Benedict XVI. Ratzinger ordered the publishers to burn all copies remaining in their warehouse. Dr Lavinia Byrne, well-known as a broadcaster, lecturer and theologian, has refused to make a public declaration of her adherence to

---

[74] Cited in ENI *Bulletin*, 24, 4 December 1996.

papal statements restricting the Catholic priesthood to men. 'I have a very serious question about how the Vatican deals with dissent' she has said. She described the Congregation of the Doctrine of the Faith as 'a faceless bureaucracy condemning individuals without hearing their story or point of view'.[75]

In the opinion of Andrea de Carvalho, an Australian Catholic laywoman, women would be good priests and leaders because they are known to consult, network, gather, share and discuss:

> We are participatory by nature. In my experience, the official Church... does not always operate in this way... We have a church that espouses to work for the alienated and the marginalised, but some women in the church, who in all other realms are deemed to be mainstream, have been made to feel like outsiders, or secondary to men. Division breeds hurt and hatred when we would rather work towards understanding and friendship.[76]

Sexism cannot be overcome if men are not prepared to accept women as equal partners. In Christianity, love is meant to be the cement that holds the community together. But, if the male half of Christian communities regards their female members as inferior, subordinates rather than partners, as the bulk of Christian membership does still,

---

[75] Cited in *Church Times*, 14 January 2000.
[76] Cited in *Catholic Voice*, June 1997.

church leaders who preach about loving one another are failing to point out that love on unequal terms is not the quality love proclaimed by Christ.

Clearly, such reform will entail a drastic paradigm shift, requiring a new basis from which to formulate moral theology and ecclesiology. Equality of women and men in the sight of God must become a central concern, with leadership being separated from the concept of 'domination over'. This will require a deconstruction of the patriarchal model which has its replacement with a new paradigm based on mutuality.

5

The Embodiment Problem

As noted in previous chapters, women have been socialised by religious and societal leaders to play subordinate roles. Churchwomen's bodies have been regulated to fit in the subsidiary spaces within ecclesial structures which male bodies, especially those wearing the insignia of high office, are reluctant to occupy. Church ethicists seldom criticise the injustice of this situation, perhaps seeing it as their duty to uphold the orthodoxy of the ecclesial system in which they work, even when the system is blatantly discriminatory.

For years, children attending mainstream churches were socialised to accept that, in Christianity, human beings in male bodies take precedence over those in female form. They observed that the majority of those who carry out proceedings in the sanctuary are male. Females are more involved in Sunday school activities, kitchens, choirs, organ playing and money raising activities.

In Christian worship today, it is still the patriarchs rather than the matriarchs who are most frequently acclaimed, such as Abraham, Isaac, Jacob, Moses, David, and the male apostles. Sarah, Rebecca, Rachel, Miriam, Hannah, Deborah and Mary Magdalene, for example, are seldom accorded the status of the men of their particular era. Nor are women saints as venerated as male saints, despite their sufferings and personal efforts to foster the growth of Christianity. It is the Virgin Mary, Jesus' mother, who receives most reverence among the biblical foremothers, and her eternally youthful motherhood, represented prolifically in art and statues, is promoted as the embodiment of an ideal Christian woman.

According to Bishop John Spong, 'the popular suggestion that devotion to Mary was translated into enhanced status for women is simply without historical evidence'. He points out that 'there is no historical correlation between the cult of the Virgin and increased status for women that can be substantiated in Western history. Mother Church was, in fact, ruled by men; and Mary served the desires of those men who created this holy ideal of what they thought all women should be and then imposed it on their women.'[77]

The valorisation of male bodies has signalled to Christian women that being female is of lesser spiritual significance. For centuries, women have been taught to worship, pray and interpret Scripture and doctrine in masculine ways, while at the same time, men have been socialised to repress the feminine within themselves. But, as theologian Sandra

---

[77] J. S. Spong, 'Women: Less than Free in Christ's Church', in Marie-Louise Uhr (ed.), *Changing Women, Changing Church*, Millennium Books, Newtown, 1992, p. 74.

Schneiders points out, 'there can be no doubt that this experience of God as male with its logical conclusions, has been negative in the extreme':

> First, women's sense of being not among the truly Godlike has preserved in women, much more than in men, the sense of the utter 'otherness' and non-controllability of God. Women have little tendency to attempt to present themselves as God's vicar, or to speak in God's name. Women are frequently much more sensitive to the reality of God's actual and free intervention in their lives. Women are often more ready to appeal to God for help and believe that God can and will respond.[78]

Because of the long exclusion of women from intellectual pursuits in general, and especially from philosophy and theology, there is a tendency among academics in these fields of study to assume that gender is not an issue. In her work *The Bodies of Women: Ethics, Embodiment and Sexual Difference*, social philosopher Roslyn Diprose observes that 'in focussing on moral principles and moral judgements the assumption is that individuals are present as self-transparent, isolated, rational minds' and that 'embodied differences between individuals are inconsequential'.[79] The

---

[78] Sandra M. Schneiders, 'The Effects of Women's Experience on their Spirituality', in Joann W. Cohn (ed.), *Women's Spirituality*, Paulist Press. New York 1986, p. 43.
[79] R. Diprose, *The Bodies of Women: Ethics, Embodiment and Sexual Difference*, Routledge, London, 1994, p. 18.

reality is that in the predominantly male-dominated world which still exists today, embodiment, male or female, is a crucial element in how intellectual output is evaluated in both church and society.

'Rational minds' have been for centuries associated with male persons, who undoubtedly promoted this concept in order to control the thought worlds of both religious and secular societies. The assumption that only male perspectives had credibility led to the automatic undervaluation of the intellectual and artistic output of women. For a major part of the last two millennia, women have been denied access to higher educational institutions in general and to theological colleges in particular, the rationale being that female minds are by nature inadequate for academia and too remote from the divine to formulate theology.

Women have been socialised to serve men, not to compete with them. Male rhetoric effectively propagated theories regarding female inferiority, most often using references to the main biological differences between men and women, namely women's functions of menstruation, child birth and lactation. Much adverse comment has been made over the centuries about women's emotional instability and irrationality, especially during premenstrual and post-natal periods, and as a result of the menopause, while the equally debilitating physical, emotional and psychological problems experienced by men have been downplayed.

The male mind has been institutionalised as superior in every way to that of the female, while female biological differences were cited to prove that a woman was intrinsically inadequate for church leadership, even at times when women were undertaking secular leadership and achieving success. For centuries, female bodies were legalised as commodities under male control, by both church and state, rather than as independent self-sufficient entities. The force of such bias, reinforced by the economic and legal powerlessness of women, has made it difficult in the past for exceptionally talented females to gain the recognition they deserved.

Women of outstanding intelligence have always existed, though opportunities to become widely recognised were limited. Through the various periods of the last two millennia, a number of exceptionally talented women have managed to overcome daunting educational and gender barriers to make outstanding contributions to the theology, literature, music and art of Christian churches. Only recently has the brilliance of female theologians such as Hildegarde of Bingen and Julian of Norwich been rediscovered, although they both enjoyed renown during their lifetimes.[80] The daring of Elizabeth Cady Stanton in writing the *Women's Bible* in the late nineteenth century enabled women to read Scripture from a different, less androcentric perspective.

The scholarship and actions of outstandingly talented female Christians tend to enjoy short periods of recognition and then fade into near oblivion, because it is not in male interests to promote them. Churchmen have been quick to rebuke women who stepped outside their prescribed roles

---

[80] Hildegarde of Bingen (1098-1179) was abbess of Rupertsberg in Germany. Julian of Norwich (b. 1343) was an English mystic and theologian.

for fear such behaviour would endanger traditional male-female relationships. Similarly, in the secular world, many women have had to assume male identities, and even clothe their bodies in male attire, to gain recognition for their work, examples being novelists Georges Sand, George Eliot, Miles Franklin and Henry Handel Richardson.

Hiding one's femininity to gain recognition in the public world of men was not necessarily affirming for women. Constance Jordan, in her work *Renaissance Feminism*, states that 'the virile woman tended to reaffirm patriarchal values'. Her excellence was seen in her masculinity - that is, her rationality, courage, and physical strength. The problem always has been to affirm the positive character of femininity, and detach it from its negative reflection in the effeminate male or 'in the misogynist caricature of woman as vain, capricious, self-indulgent, garrulous, and stupid'.[81]

Constance Jordan found from her research that feminists in sixteenth century Europe began to argue for the worth of femininity, represented by mercy, patience and temperance, and its value in society as a whole to offset 'degenerate masculinity – the cruelty typical of the tyrant or bully – with deleterious effects on the family and the state'.[82]

Men for centuries gathered wisdom from women and presented it to the world as the product of their own intellect. Men have always approved of women as their helpers and advisers, yet they have been reluctant to acknowledge publicly women's contributions to their achievements. When

---

[81] Constance Jordan, *Renaissance Feminism: Literary Texts and Political Models*, Cornell University Press, Ithaca, 1990, p. 137.
[82] *Ibid.*

women aired their ideas independently, rather than behind a male facade, they frequently incurred disapproval or denigration. Admittedly, women could be as scathing of their sisters' intellectual output as were men, having been socialised to believe that intellectual pursuits were not part of the female sphere. Church leaders, as the records show, particularly disliked churchwomen to shine in areas which were regarded as male reserves, fearing an emasculation of their sacred male system. Clergy disapproval of women could be waspish and trivial, including snide remarks about styles of dress, jewellery and cosmetics. New fashions could draw forth adverse comment, especially when women first appeared in church in trousers rather than skirts, and when they abandoned their hats and veils. As 'wearing the pants' was a phrase associated with authority in the Western world, women in trousers, no matter how stylish and decorative the material and design, were perceived as posing a challenge to the patriarchal order. As one Australian Roman Catholic priest recently commented in a sermon, 'the Church's present problems began when women appeared in bifurcated skirts!'.

If one browses through church newspapers of the twentieth century, one will discover increasing clergy concern about women emerging from their private secluded habitat into the public arena. For example, in 1939, an Australian Anglican cleric, Bishop Hart of Wangaratta Diocese, wrote several articles criticising the increasing independence of twentieth-century women, claiming that 'the needs of today will not be met by manlike women. The real need is that men shall know women to be – that women shall feel themselves to be – not daughters of Eve but children of Mary'.[83] Bishop Hart was indicating that women who did not conform to their traditional roles and conservative fashions in dress were automatically moving in the direction of sinfulness. But in 1939, World War II broke out and, for the next six years, many churchwomen trained for and carried out jobs previously reserved for men in order to address national shortages of labour. During this period, women demonstrated that they were capable of doing more than the tasks traditionally assigned to females.

Churchmen's ingrained lack of respect for women became startlingly evident when the issue of women's ordination to priesthood was first raised in the early twentieth century. Extraordinary statements about women, quite out of step with the bland remarks usually expressed by clergy, were aired. In the Australian Anglican Church, an example of the deep revulsion some clergy experienced at the thought of women becoming priests was evident in the remark by the Rev. Ian Herring of Victoria that 'it would be analogous to consecrating a meat pie on the altar of God to ordain a woman'.[84] This somewhat irrational statement suggested that Herring considered the female embodiment of priesthood could change the elements of the Eucharist!

Now, in the Third Millennium, the number of tertiary educated women entering the workforce is increasing, especially in the Christian West. Clearly, women's access to a broader range of subjects in schools and their entry to higher education has played a crucial role in dispelling the

---

[83] *The Church Chronicle*, Brisbane, October 1939.
[84] See M. Rose, *Freedom from Sanctified Sexism: Women Transforming the Church*, Allira Publications, MacGregor, Queensland, 1996, p. 198, fn. 67.

myth that brain power and technical skills are confined to the male sex. Indeed, the fact that girls are outperforming boys educationally has triggered a male backlash. Programs are being devised in schools to improve the performance of boys.

As women succeed in attaining improved recognition in society generally, they expect a similar rise in status to take place in church environments. Churchwomen are actively seeking ways to avoid inscription into traditional female identities, which limited the senior church positions open to them in the past. In the centuries when male minds dominated both religious and secular affairs, women were forced to accept passivity in church and society, sometimes under the threat of harsh punishment if they challenged their inferior status. Women were frustratedly aware that they did not possess the depth of knowledge to argue their case convincingly. Most women also lacked the economic means to break loose from the male privileged system which confined them, and where they had little opportunity to develop their non-domestic talents. Those were the years when property laws were framed to prevent women from achieving financial independence.

The process of challenging male dominance has been a thorny path for women, especially in the pioneering stages. For women entering academia in the late nineteenth and early twentieth century, it was almost imperative to accept the normative masculine style of procedures and written expression, rather than try to introduce an innovative female approach. Conformity with the long-established male traditions appeared to be the compromise women needed to make to gain recognition, and perhaps why those few women following scholarly pursuits were stereotyped as 'unfeminine'. As women gained confidence in their abilities and increased numbers undertook tertiary education, they began to articulate their thoughts and research findings in ways which were much less inhibited by male norms, projecting their unique perspective.

Despite the fact that the female body was perceived as being of lesser significance, women recognised that they must dare to draw attention to their embodied selves in order to prevent assimilation into the male generic shroud which enveloped so much of academia. As Elizabeth Grosz comments in her book *Volatile Bodies*: 'Our conceptions of reality, knowledge, truth, politics, ethics and aesthetics are all effects of sexually specific – and thus far in our history usually male – bodies, and are all thus implicated in the power structures which feminists have described as patriarchal, the structures which govern relations between the sexes'.[85] She continues:

> The subject, recognised as a corporeal being, can no longer readily succumb to the neutralization and neutering of its specificity which has occurred to women as a consequence of women's submersion under male definition. The body is the ally of sexual difference, a key term in questioning the centrality of a number of benign but nonetheless phallocentric presumptions

---

[85] E. Grosz, *Volatile Bodies: Toward a Corporeal Feminism*, Allen and Unwin, St. Leonards, 1994, p. ix.

which have hidden the cultural and intellectual effacement of women.[86]

There is contention between women on whether the naked female body can be used as a powerful Christian symbol because women's bodies have been so much identified as the antithesis of the spiritual in Western Christianity. Female nakedness is so much associated with sexual arousal in Christianity that it will be difficult to ascribe spiritual significance to it. Certainly, two artistic depictions of women on the Cross, Edwina Sandy's 'Christa' and Arthur Boyd's 'Crucifixion Shoalhaven', have caused both adverse and positive comment in Christian churches. 'Christa' was placed for some time in the Episcopal Cathedral of Saint John the Divine in New York City and has been identified with Christ's suffering for *all* humanity.

Margaret Miles expressed reservations about 'Christa' in her work *Carnal Knowing*:

> As a private devotional image, it may have great healing potential for women who have themselves been battered or raped. Yet as a public image... there are fundamental problems with the image. The *Christa*, by its visual association with the crucified Christ, glorifies the suffering of women in a society in which violence against woman has reached epidemic proportions. Equally disturbing is its association with pornography, which similarly fetishes

[86] *Ibid*.

suffering women. The naked and tortured female body has been appropriated by a media culture and cannot therefore be arbitrarily assigned religious meaning.[87]

Seyla Benhabib, in her work *Situating the Self*, concludes that the exclusion of women's experience from moral theorising is due to the disembodied concept of the moral self in the theories formulated, in that human relations are viewed from the male perspective.[88] In terms of the doctrines and moral theologies which are presently preventing women from holding office in the Vatican and Orthodox Patriarchates, female embodiment is of major concern. The active bodily presence of women among top level decision-making males (many celibate) will be an essential means of attacking the systemic causes of biological alienation.

In the twentieth century, as university education became more accessible to women, and their academic achievements proved that they possessed intellectual ability, there was inevitably a male backlash. In the mid-1970s, I remember that there were several married female students in my year who felt pressured to drop out of their studies because of the resentment they were experiencing from husbands who took umbrage at having wives who were better educated than they were. These women sacrificed their self-enhancement for the sake of holding their families together and for fear of the economic deprivation of a broken marriage. Similarly,

---

[87] Margaret M. Miles, *Carnal Knowing*, p. 177
[88] S. Benhabib, *Situating the Self: Gender, Community and Post-modernism in Contemporary Ethics*, Polity Press, Cambridge, 1992, p. 152.

I remember a woman deacon who chose not to proceed to priesthood because her husband believed in the doctrine of 'male headship' and so would be offended if she had priestly authority.

According to American Episcopal theologians, Beverley Harrison and Carter Heyward, 'in Christianity woman is equated with flesh, body, but Christian women have no integrity of embodied selfhood; no authoritative voice in determining where we put our bodies/ourselves, with whom we share our bodies/ourselves, where we put our embodied energies, time and talents.' Harrison and Heyward point out that 'women in Christianity are meant to live for others'.[89]

Certainly, in the first half of the twentieth century, there have been examples of clergy advising women not to undertake higher education or, if they do, advising them to use their skills in the service of their family or for church mission rather than in the public sphere.[90] 'Selfishness' in women has been regarded as a major sin. In men, selfishness is often condoned, interpreted as good sense and perfectly acceptable behaviour because society has taught the male that he is entitled to be waited upon by women and to expect his wishes to receive priority. As a result, churchwomen are made to feel guilty if they put their own needs and desires before those of others, particularly if those 'others' are male.

---

[89] Beverley W. Harrison/Carter Heyward, 'Pain and Pleasure: Avoiding the Confusions of Christian Tradition in Feminist Theory', in Joanne C. Brown and Carole Bohn (eds). *Christianity, Patriarchy and Abuse: A Feminist Critique*, The Pilgrim Press, New York, 1989, pp. 157-8.

[90] See, for example, *Church Chronicle*, Brisbane, 4 January 1913.

Men communicated in the past by the code of authority and women by the code of subordination. The increasing entry of women into executive positions in the twenty first century has triggered off a re-coding process which it is hoped will eliminate the assumption that the male voice is of greater significance. Women are gaining confidence in what they are saying, and the media has helped them to get their message across. Women have to remind themselves continually that they have always been as intellectually talented and rational as men. It was just that in the past their ideas were not considered worthy of consideration until they had been repeated by male lips or written into male-authored texts.

According to feminist researcher, Dr Dale Spender, while the old code still predominates, 'some men are breaking the code – they let us finish, they consult us, they draw us into conversation and ask us what we think'. But she acknowledges that 'other men are still very uncomfortable with women being consulted'.[91]

For centuries, women have been located in Christian communities which, for them are ethically confusing. They become aware that double standards exist. Churchmen are not expected to conform as strictly to Christian ethical codes in their daily lives as are women. In Australia, there have been recent examples of parish clergy and even a diocesan bishop being allowed to continue their ministry although being reprimanded for having had extramarital affairs. In a culture where men tend to condone the sexual exploits and philandering of their male associates, a clergyman is

---

[91] Cited in *Courier Mail*, 4 April 2000.

inhibited from condemning such practices too vigorously for fear of being labelled 'a wowser' or 'old maid'. Clergy have a tendency to cover up other clergy's indiscretions, even when these have traumatised young children. However, drawing attention to women's sexual misdemeanours is culturally very acceptable behaviour in male circles, and clergymen have had no qualms in the past about labelling women as 'whores' if they infringe the codes relating to sexual relations.

Even in hymns to female saints, which one might expect to be adulatory, women have been denigrated, as Leonie Liveris has discovered in her research on women in Orthodoxy. She cites the findings of Eva Catafygioutu Topping:

> Even Orthodoxy's female saints did not entirely escape the stigma of their gender. Hymns written in honour of women saints document the durability of our sexist tradition. In the corpus of Greek hymns to women saints, there is hardly one that does not denigrate the female sex. They contained innumerable references to 'female weakness', the 'shame of women' and the 'rottenness of female nature'.[92]

In the notorious fifteenth century handbook for the regulation of witches, *Malleus Maleficarum*, women were categorised as inherently defective and satanic. Many of

---

[92] Eva C. Topping, *Holy Mothers of Orthodoxy*, Life and Light Publishing, Minneapolis, 1987, p. 62, cited in L. Liveris, 'Time to Speak', p. 200.

the instruments of torture used on women suspected of witchcraft were directed towards female genitalia, the breast and vagina.

Demonisation of the 'female' has been psychologically empowering for Christian men, sanctifying male hegemony. Churchmen have been socialised to believe that the male and his thought world are closest to the mind of God. They have for centuries been allowed the sole right to theologise from pulpits and platforms. Preaching to a captive congregation has allowed countless male clerics access to linguistic weaponry with which to terrorise women into accepting subordination.

The last two centuries have witnessed the emergence of women's movements aimed at rejecting entrenched attitudes which are disadvantageous for females. Certainly, the Christian women's liberation movement, in its multiple forms, has met with solid opposition from churchmen and has been in many instances declared heretical or equated with Satan. Church leaders have long regarded women's efforts to share authority as 'unclean power', which they try to control through edicts and religious law.[93] Nevertheless, the entry of women into ordained ministry in Protestant, Anglican and Old Catholic churches has provided role models of female bodies in sanctuaries and pulpits, acting as spiritual leaders, including holding the office of bishop.

---

[93] For interesting comments on this topic, see Kim Power, 'Heavenly Bodies, The Ambiguity of the Body in Religious Discourse and Practice', Junior Charles Strong Trust Lecture 1997, delivered at the 22nd Annual Conference of the Australian Association for the Study of Religions, Brisbane, July 1997, p. 19.

When women's bodies are accorded religious significance and are acknowledged to be worthy of the offices they hold, then the issue of male supremacy can no longer be sustained as being necessary to God's order, nor can the argument of male only succession be regarded as relevant to priesthood.

Reporting on her impressions of the Second European Ecumenical Assembly in Graz in March 1997, Mihaela Rabu of the Romanian Orthodox Church observed that the physical absence of women is conducive to male-centred decision-making:

> On the last day I heard someone who attended the last press conference saying: 'Here are two parallel worlds, one of the men in the Plenary Hall and one of the women's world... I just wonder if women's voices were really heard by the hierarchies of the Churches and if they will listen. Also, I wonder if when decisions are made, those who design the decisions are really thinking of all the people'.[94]

This remark is backed by my own research on reports from male-only synods in the Australian Anglican Church during the first half of the twentieth century in particular, where women's activities barely rated a mention, despite the important role women played in church expansion, mission and maintaining economic viability.[95] The same could be

---

[94] Mihaela Rabu, 'Women Do Ecumenism: Impressions from the Second European Ecumenical Assembly in Graz', *MaryMartha*, International Orthodox Women's Journal, Vol. 5, No. 2, Winter/Spring 1997, p. 24.

[95] See Mavis Rose, *Freedom from Sanctified Sexism*.

said about many of the statements and documents issuing from the male-only commissions of the Vatican and from the Orthodox Patriarchates.[96] Demetria Velisarios Jaquet, a member of the Armenian Orthodox Church, has expressed her disquiet about the continuing exclusion of women:

> Many current gender issues are in fact age-old moral and ethical questions about treating each other as persons instead of objects ... Is the theology of the Fathers truly egalitarian, or does it in fact express that there is a fundamental difference between men and women...? Do they describe reality or just social practice? Are they descriptive in an open-ended way, inviting the spontaneity of the Spirit? Or are they prescriptively pointing to an authentic bottom line that may not be moved.[97]

It is these boundaries, the 'immovable bottom line' and the 'stained glass ceiling', which churchwomen today are challenging. There is increasing recognition that the forces opposing gender equality in Christianity have had a malign influence on society generally. Excessive male power tends to go hand in hand with excessive aggression, which so often leads to violent conflict. Women believe that a less damaged planet might result from more balanced gender relations, benefitting men as well as women.

---

[96] Examples of such statements by Roman Catholic and Orthodox leaders have been cited in previous chapters.
[97] Demetria Velisarios Jaquet, 'Sexuality and the Church', in *MaryMartha*, Vol. 5, 1997, pp. 26-27.

One of the problems of the moral theology expounded in the oldest Christian churches, especially Roman Catholicism and Orthodoxy, is the narrow, exclusive way in which ethical reflection takes place. Can a balanced ethical stance be formulated when half the church members, i.e. women, have minimum input into deliberations on moral issues? Moral theology needs to be constructed on principles of gender mutuality and inclusiveness. Major church leaders have had a tendency to regard women's bodily functions unfavourably. Menstruating and post-natal women were regarded as being unclean and birth control using contraceptives is still frowned upon by the Vatican.

Diprose argues that ethics is about 'location, position and place' and that one's habitual way of life, *ethos*, determines ones' character or 'specificity'. She is of the opinion that:

> From this understanding of ethos, *ethics can be defined as the study and practice of that which constitutes one's habitat*, or as the problematic of the constitution of one's embodied place in the world.[98]

Diprose supports an ethical viewpoint which recognises a 'constitutive relation between one's world (habitat) and one's embodied character (ethos)'.[99] For women, this means that their bodies and minds should be interacting mutually with those of males in deciding the relevant moral standards for their community, including their religious environment.

---

[98] R. Diprose, *The Bodies of Women*, pp. 18-19.
[99] *Ibid.*

Priests in Roman Catholicism, and to some degree in the Orthodox churches, have an unusual habitat in that they practise celibacy and so are not permitted to cohabit in an intimate, sensual way with women. When a person is religiously dedicated to a lifestyle which is devoid of close physical contact with women, it is easy to understand how women's embodiment is either ignored in deliberations or else used as an object of moral discourse in a habitat which has socialised its members against the corruptive influence of the female body. The female body for celibate male clergy is so closely aligned to 'forbidden fruit' that it would be difficult for them to accord the female body/self an authoritative place in the formulation of moral theology. Roman Catholic clergy have had to suffer the pain of frustrated libidos, their main compensation being the prestige the Church has accorded to those males willing to exclude themselves from cohabitation with women.[100]

According to Riane Eisler in her work *Sacred Pleasure*, 'the Church's "moral" condemnation of sexuality was far more than a psychological quirk', it was a political strategy to impose and maintain its control as the one and only faith and thus consolidate its power.[101] Thus the natural habitat or *ethos* of male clerics and men in religious orders was robbed of gender balance in order to make Christianity different

---

[100] Kim Power (see reference 94) points out that 'in Greek society, a married man expected to sleep with his wife for the sake of producing citizens for the city-state, but ideally his purest love would be directed towards men, because true love could only exist between moral equals.' See 'Heavenly Bodies', p. 5.

[101] Riane Eisler, *Sacred Pleasure: Sex, Myth and the Politics of the Body*, Doubleday, 1976, pp. 30-31.

from earlier religious traditions which associated sexuality with the spiritual and the divine.

Not only has the habitat of women been undervalued, but it has not been historically recorded. Church historiographers have dispossessed women by writing histories centred on prominent churchmen. Church history tends to be divided into papal or episcopal regimes, where the focus is on the interaction between senior clerics, theologians, prominent laymen and politicians. The message which women receive from church history is that their contribution to their church and society has been too insignificant to record. Whenever mention has been made about churchwomen, it has most often concerned their roles as wives of ruling churchmen or as generous benefactors. The deeds of outstanding nuns or female missionaries may also be recorded, though usually in special works rather than general church history.

Female embodiment in future church histories will prevent women's submersion under male definition. As Ann Dworkin comments:

> There are no disembodied processes ... all history originates in human flesh...all oppression is inflicted by the body of one against the body of another... all social change is built on the bone and muscle, and out of the flesh and blood, of human creatures.[102]

---
[102] A. Dworkin, *Our Blood*, The Women's Press, New York, 1976, p. 82.

Today, Christian women are trying to recover their past, using oral sources and occasional reports on women which were never integrated into mainstream church documentation but stored separately in church archives. But separate male and female histories seldom produce balanced records. Church history in the future needs to include both male and female embodiment to make it more authentic.

The situation in the field of theology has been similar. As pointed out previously, there were early female theologians whose works simply gained fleeting recognition until recently rediscovered. Maria Bingemer points out that 'in theological production, the past for women was marked by centuries of absence as practitioners, and by a deep silence':

> Until recently, there were in the history of theology no books or articles written by women, no courses run by women, no chairs occupied by women. No-one even bothered to specify the sex of the authors of theological texts or of professors of theology. It was obvious that such work was a male prerogative.[103]

The two major Christian churches have retained up to the present time doctrines which insist that only a male body is appropriate to represent Christ sacramentally. For example, highly respected theologian Thomas Aquinas wrote in Summa, I, 93, 41: 'God's image is found in man in a way that is not verified in woman'. Aquinas believed in

---

[103] Maria C. Bingemer, 'Women in the Future of the Theology of Liberation' in M. Ellis and O. Maduro (eds), *The Future of Liberation Theology*, Orbis, New York, 1989, pp. 18-19.

an 'eminence of degree', meaning a superiority by nature. It was not possible, in his view, for the female sex to signify eminence of degree, for a woman was by nature in a state of subjection.

Sexual resemblance to Jesus Christ became an important criterion for church leadership, especially in the less Protestant denominations. Veronique Lossky, an Orthodox theologian, has commented that 'the iconic value of Christ is, for the moment, a real stumbling block for women' because when they discuss with church leaders the future entry of women into priesthood, the reply received is that women are automatically disqualified because 'the priest who presides at the Eucharist represents Christ' and 'Christ became incarnate as a man.'[104] These statements, as we have discussed previously, ignore the theological reality that Christ represented all humanity, women as well as men, and that it is the bread and wine which represent Christ, while the presiding priest represents the church members, male and female, known as the Body of Christ. The church body has consistently been more female than male in its regular worship attendance.

The denigration of women, both their minds and their bodies, has been one of Christianity's most enduring unethical, abusive actions. It has been a nullification of Christ's commandment to love all people because love which requires the loved one to be subordinate is automatically flawed and self-interested. Scant concern has been shown for the adverse effects on women's confidence and self-esteem

---

[104] V. Lossky, 'Women's Ministry – from an Orthodox point of view. A re-reading', *MaryMartha*, Vol. 5, No. 2, Winter/Spring 1997, p. 74.

as a result of being categorised en masse as unsubstantial nonentities, born to serve and service men. It becomes more difficult for women to relate intimately to a Father God who, they are taught, views as second-rate the female body which encompasses their being and who prefers women to occupy their habitat as unobtrusively as possible.

Women have to keep stressing the biblical fact that they too were created in the likeness of God. Certainly, the male *imago Dei* concept, like the myth of the rational male mind, is so deeply entrenched in Christianity that it is difficult to uproot. The *imago Dei* concept, like many other Christian doctrines, was not received directly from Jesus Christ. Roman patriarchal influences impacted strongly on the Early Church. To Roman men of power and authority, the Senate would present a wax image, an *imago*, of their own likeness. It was a privilege accorded to free men only. As Kim Power points out in her article on heavenly bodies, 'one can see why Roman Christians had such difficulty in according to women the dignity of the *imago Dei*'.[105]

Of course, there are other ways to represent Christ. One could argue that women have, by their 'being-for-others', always closely resembled Jesus Christ the Good Shepherd, Comforter and Healer. Women's pastoral and missionary commitment has been an equally valid image of Christ. Jesus not only encouraged women to go out and proclaim his message, but he endorsed the humanly inclusive rite of baptism to celebrate initiation into his movement, rejecting the Jewish male-only rite of circumcision.

---

[105] Kim Power, 'Heavenly Bodies, p. 14.

The problem for Christianity is that it never succeeded in withstanding the cultural trends which demeaned women in the milieux in which it first put down roots. Worship of the male body was present in the Mediterranean region before the coming of Jesus Christ. In the first century BCE, phallic cults proliferated in Greece and Rome, with close links between religion, sexuality, and power.[106] The ideal physical body had religio-cultural values. The adulation of the male body resulted in it acquiring a godlike dimension. Phallic amulets were tied around children's necks to keep them safe, only discarded at puberty. Male babies were valued; female infanticide or the sale of young females into slavery was common – practices which are still alive in several cultures in the world today although not sanctioned by Christian churches.

Graeco-Roman gender perspectives impacted strongly on Palestinian colonial society during the first century. That Jesus was able to resist so strongly the male-dominant influences surrounding him and to treat women with dignity was a sign of his determination to show that all people, irrespective of race, gender and class, were entitled to love and honour. Jesus revealed to the world a God whose domain was based on love in community, surely the highest form of ethos. Leadership in the Jesus movement was shared, based on talent rather than on gender. The emphasis was on a 'discipleship of equals'. This ethos cut across the religious and societal structures of Jesus' day.

In first Century Jewish society, contact with the human body was taboo when it was ritually unclean or leprous.

---

[106] These topics are widely discussed in Kim Power, 'Heavenly Bodies'.

Jesus challenged bodily taboos, removing the yoke of alienation from those deemed to be untouchable. For example, as Simon Peter's mother-in-law lay sick with fever, Jesus took her by the hand, a break with religious custom. (Mark 1:29-31). He gave encouragement to the woman with an ongoing menstrual problem, praising her for her faith rather than chiding her for being religiously polluting. The woman felt in her body that she had been made whole through physical contact with Jesus (Mark 5:24-34). These incidents among many indicated that Jesus was committed to removing cultural barriers which discriminated against bodies in need of care, especially relieving the situation for women.

The reality in Christianity in the Third Millennium is that major church leaders are still clinging to the tradition that women are basically inadequate for leadership because they do not occupy male bodies. The injustice of excluding Roman Catholic and Orthodox women from central decision-making processes and from admission to the priesthood by virtue of their embodiment, continues today. One can understand why churchmen, especially those who have risen to the pinnacles of power, are reluctant to dispense with the 'male only' requirement for priesthood. It is a potent ego-booster for churchmen to be told that their genitalia accord them a special affinity with God. Churchmen have for two thousand years gained immense spiritual satisfaction from the belief that the male body represents the divine and the female body the frail human. Exultation of maleness is an enduring tradition in Christianity. Divinity is constantly proclaimed in male form in Scripture readings, hymns and liturgies. Male adulation can also be found in reports and church newspapers, the following extract from a poem, which appeared in the Australian Anglican *Church Chronicle* in 1948, being an example:

> Give us men,
> Men whose lives reflect the beauty
> Of the saints of olden time;
> Men who know and do their duty
> As from rock to rock they climb.
> If they stumble, born of woman,
> All the humbler, all the stronger,
> Haply struggling on the longer,
> Not angelic, nobly human,
> Very men of flesh and blood,
> Yet of heaven's own brotherhood.[107]

The poem suggests that male 'flesh and blood' is not carnal like women's; it is 'nobly human'. The only reference to women in the poem is derogatory – if men stumble, it is because they cannot avoid being 'born of woman'. The reference to 'heaven's own brotherhood' suggests that, eschatologically, men will continue to have privileged status.

The doctrine of the Trinity proclaims an androcentric concept of Godhead, with two male embodied figures, the Father and the Son, and a Holy Spirit, which one would assume to be disembodied and genderless, but who in the Nicene Creed is referred to as 'the Lord and giver of life'. The Trinitarian Doctrine, as formulated, therefore enshrines a male habitat, which excludes the female *imago Dei*. Of

---

[107] *The Church Chronicle*, September 1948.

course, theologically, Godhead transcends human familial categorisation, so the Doctrine of the Trinity is metaphorical. Only Jesus Christ can be identified as having been an embodied person.

There have been some efforts in Christianity to respond to women's concerns about their devaluation by the Church. Many Christian churches have removed regulations and liturgies based on Hebrew purification rites in regard to females, although Orthodox women are still chafing against continued church practices which infer that the female body is not as ritually pure as that of the male. An example of this discrimination is the prolonged period before churching of female babies can take place and their exclusion from the sanctuary. We have also previously noted that women cannot receive the Eucharistic sacraments during their menstruation period.

At an Orthodox workshop on 'Men and Women in the Church' held in 1997, a group of young girls queried their exclusion from the sanctuary since young males were encouraged to be there, arguing: 'If the sanctuary is a holy place, boys should not go in there either, as they are just as sinful as girls?'[108] A priest's daughter protested because she was not allowed to assist her father when no boy acolyte was present.

At the present time, the Vatican is behaving ambivalently, trying to retract the gains made for women at the Second Vatican Council, while at the same time softening the blow by assuring women that they are valued as long as

---

[108] See V. Lossky, 'Report of the Workshop on "Men and Women in the Church"', in *MaryMartha*, Vol. 5, No. 2, Winter/Spring, 1997, pp. 34-35.

they adhere to the obedient, intercessory model of the Virgin Mary. Vatican II proclaimed the equal status of men and women, critiquing the entrenched male supremacist traditions, thus opening the way for trained women to hold any office in the Church. The Pontifical Biblical Commission added further strength to the statement by voting (12-5) in April 1975 that Christ's will would not be violated by allowing women to be ordained.[109] Since Vatican II, conservative forces within the Catholic Church have been intent on shutting the door on power sharing with women.

Christianity has been so successful in isolating sexuality from God's kingdom, that to achieve gender balance, there needs to be a new theology which identifies intimacy between the sexes, both bodily and soulfully, as an acceptable, sanctified element of life. Women are no longer prepared to wait around while theologians speculate on how to resolve religious gender issues. Women are claiming the right to decision-making concerning their own bodies, acting according to their own consciences. Many Roman Catholic lay women are ignoring papal injunctions forbidding the use of contraceptive devices or IVF technology, and are receiving support from sympathetic nuns and priests at the grassroots level. Ecologically, birth control is an important issue as overpopulation is a major problem in sustaining the Earth and its natural resources.

That women are taking independent stances on ethical and theological issues alarms many churchmen, putting

---

[109] See B. A. Asen, 'Women and the Ministerial Priesthood: An Annotated Bibliography', *Theology Digest*, 29:4, Winter, 1981, pp. 329-342.

them on the defensive. Michael Korda believes that male fear of women may lie at the heart of patriarchy. He comments:

> There has always been, in men, an instinctive fear...that women are in fact a more successful artefact of nature than men. The complexity of their biology, their miraculous ability to give birth to another human being, the early impact of a mother's power on every man, all conspire to produce in men a slight feeling of awe about the potentials of women once they are unleashed.[110]

As history reveals, the male body has also found it difficult to live without access to a female body. Female prostitution has been an area where the Church has been vocal, again the guilt being directed towards women rather than the males whose demand for brothels has kept the sex trade alive. Scant attention has been drawn to the economic factors involved, in particular the family pressures which force young women into prostitution and pornography. Mary Hunt, Director of Women's Alliance for Theology, Ethics and Ritual, has been critical of the failure of church leaders to support these women, commending:

> I characterise the contemporary ethical reflections from the Vatican (and related ecclesial institutions, though I do not consider it

---

[110] M. Korda, *Male Chauvinism*, Hodder and Stoughton, London, 1975, p. 148.

ecumenically polite to critique them) as nothing short of theological pornography.[111]

Pornography focuses abusively on women's bodies. One could claim that church fathers, by denigrating female bodies since the second century, have projected a subtle suggestion that women's bodies are expendable. Churchwomen have been urged to act as the guardians of purity in sexual intercourse, but males have been given much more freedom to indulge in sexual harassment and exploitation of women.

A reflection in 1978 by Rev. Bruce Wilson, until recently Australian Anglican Bishop of Bathurst but then a Sydney rector, was critical of general attitudes towards sexuality in the Church:

> Puritanism and pornography – both do dirt on sex. Both deny the warm, human, bonding effect of sexuality in all human relationships. Before the changed attitudes of the last twenty years or so, the female was expected to uphold the puritan virtues. She was expected to say 'no' to the male's sexual advances. If she didn't resist him, the man considered her to be a slut. He might spend part of the night with her, joke among his mates about 'scoring' with her – but he would never consider marrying such an unvirtuous woman. Such was the hypocrisy of

---

[111] M. E. Hunt, 'Theological Pornography: From Corporate to Communal Ethics' in J. C. Brown and C. R. Bohn, *Christianity, Patriarchy and Abuse: A Feminist Critique*, pp. 90-91.

the puritan-pornographic mentality. The true female was expected to be sexless except in her duty to provide the male his 'matrimonial rights'. 'Barefoot, pregnant and in the kitchen' was an Australian male joke not too far from the truth of the essential masculine attitude. The male was the sexual marauder.[112]

---

[112] *Church Scene*, Melbourne, 16 November 1978.

6
The Cost of Dissent

By means of his Apostolic Letter *Ad Tuendam Fidem* (For the Defence of the Faith) issued on 30 June 1998, Pope John Paul II reiterated that he was still vehemently opposed to changing Roman Catholic traditions and doctrine, despite mounting calls for reform. To quell the increasing stridency of these voices, the Magisterium chose to toughen its stance, threatening to exercise firmer control over dissidents.

Liberals have long been perceived as the triggers for unrest in mainstream Christianity. *Ad Tuendam Fidem* was especially targeted at progressive theologians and religious educators, who have largely ignored or else criticised papal injunctions to toe the orthodox line, also venturing to make suggestions about how the centralist, clericalised system of Roman Catholic government should be restructured.

The apostolic letter *Ad Tuendam Fidem* warned that the Vatican is no longer prepared to turn a blind eye towards non-compliance with its rulings, making clear that those who continued to defy them would suffer the consequences. The apostolic letter amended Canon 750 of the Code of Canon Law to include new 'just penalties' for theological dissent, not just for dissent from 'infallible' teachings but also for dissent from 'definitive' teachings.[113]

The adjective 'definitive' usually applies to teachings formally declared by a pope to be divinely revealed, and thus part of the 'deposit of faith'. Richard McBride of Notre Dame University in America pointed out that the Pope 'now seems to be insisting that non-infallible but definitive teachings are to be regarded as if they are infallible'.[114]

The Pope's apostolic letter was accompanied by a *Commentary* written by Cardinal Joseph Ratzinger (then Prefect of the Congregation for the Doctrine of the Faith, now Pope Benedict XVI) and signed by both Ratzinger and Archbishop Tarcisio Bertone, Secretary of the Congregation. In his *Commentary*, as had been his style in the past, Ratzinger interpreted the Pope's apostolic letter in a forceful manner which exceeded the severity of the papal document itself. Ratzinger stressed that 'on questions of faith and morals, the only subject qualified to fulfil the office of teaching with binding authority for the faithful is the Supreme Pontiff, with the College of Bishops in communion with him', because by divine institution they are the successors of the Apostles 'in teaching and in pastoral governance'. In other words, Ratzinger was re-affirming that the Pope and the Roman Catholic bishops exercise full control over what church

---

[113] Cited in R. McBride, 'Hammering the Liberals', in *The Tablet*, 11 July 1998, p. 900.
[114] *Ibid.*

members should believe and what should constitute their ethical stance, because they are the direct line of descent from the apostles.

Ratzinger also declared that doctrines 'contained in the Word of God, written or handed down, and defined with a solemn judgment as divinely revealed truths either by the Roman Pontiff when he speaks *ex cathedra*, or by the College of Bishops gathered in Council, or infallibly proposed', require the 'assent of theological faith by all members of the faithful'. Ratzinger warned:

> Thus, whoever obstinately places them in doubt or denies them falls under the censure of *heresy*, as indicated by the respective canons of the Codes of Canon Law.[115]

Heresy has always been a menacing word. In the past, when church and state were closely linked, holding religious opinions which were contrary to orthodoxy could be life-threatening. Admittedly, heresy charges were often more related to political, social or scientific matters than to Christian doctrine, being useful as a means of getting rid of agitators, or reducing the power of Muslims, Jews and women.

For Christians today, 'heresy' accusations may be vocationally, spiritually and emotionally disturbing, but do not incur a penalty under civil law in modern societies. Heresy charges are more likely to stimulate informal

---

[115] Cardinal Ratzinger's *Commentary* on 'For the Defence of the Faith', reproduced in *The Tablet*, 11 July 1998, pp. 920-922..

Christian dialogue concerning the ethics of strict adherence to church law, with queries whether hierarchical stifling of dissent runs contrary to the injunction by Jesus to search for truth.

Many Christians nowadays consider that enforced belief hinders the role of the Holy Spirit in awakening Christian conscience. Dissenters point out that Jesus was a visionary who subverted conventional wisdom where he saw it to be no longer relevant, or damaging for the powerless. Jesus spent much of his ministry in a state of contention with the religious hierarchy of his day, advising against rigid observance of laws which did not reflect the ethos of God's domain. Jesus' teachings and example serve as a model for the faithful to be vigilant and unafraid of dissent. In the freer religious environment that exists today, authoritarian church leaders are discovering that their decrees are less deferentially received. They also face accusations from women that God's life-giving Spirit is being usurped by oligarchies of male bishops and patriarchs.

In paragraph 3 of his *Commentary* on *Ad Tuendam Fidem*, Ratzinger conceded that Christ had promised to bestow the Holy Spirit, who 'will guide you into all truth', but he was reluctant to give credence to spiritual revelations which did not accord with views held by the Vatican. Ratzinger contended that 'other truths have to be understood more deeply before full possession can be attained of what God, in his mystery of love, wished to reveal to men for their salvation'. There was no mention in this statement that many of the new revelations under attack by the Vatican concerned the position of women in the Church.

In the opinion of Elizabeth Flamsteed, an Australian Catholic laywoman and former leader of the Southeast Queensland branch of Ordination of Catholic Women, 'the present Pope's (then John Paul II) intellectual timidity in attempting to suppress discussion of women's ordination leaves no room for the voice of the Holy Spirit to speak in the evolving Church. This unrealistic expectation further damages his credibility. His 'stand back, I'm running this show' attitude is an affront to laity who have a genuine desire to be involved in a Church grounded in equality'.[116]

As mentioned briefly in Chapter 4, Dr Lavinia Byrne, a Roman Catholic nun, defied the Vatican by speaking out boldly on the subject of women's ordination, at the same time publishing a book entitled *Women at the Altar*. The Congregation for the Doctrine of the Faith demanded that she make a public declaration of her adherence to the encyclical letter *Humanae Vitae* put out by Pope Paul VI in 1968, and to the papal document restricting priestly ordination to men. Byrne declared: 'I considered that to reduce the whole of Catholic teaching to these two documents was to trivialise the life of faith and I refused to do so'.[117]

Modern day heresy charges are not confined to Roman Catholicism. They tend to be triggered by ultra conservative church leaders. In March 1993, the Sydney presbytery of the Presbyterian Church of Australia declared Rev. Dr Peter Cameron, the warden of St Andrew's College in the University of Sydney, guilty of heresy because he had

---

[116] *Australian*, 17 October 2000.
[117] Cited in *Church Times*, 14 January 2000.

opposed the church's decision to cease ordaining women to ministry. The Sydney Presbytery declared that the matter at issue was not women's ordination but Dr Cameron's view of the authority of the Bible, in particular the texts subordinating women to men.

Cameron has written two books about his experiences of undergoing a heresy trial, *Heretic and Fundamentalism and Freedom*. He has commented:

> It is obviously not a good thing if you're a minister to have 'heretic' on your CV... To be called a heretic by one group may be considered a badge of honour in another. There are, however, few advantages in being infamous, and on the whole the status of the heretic is not one that I would recommend. There is a certain image conjured up by the word which is essentially negative; not only are you suspect theologically, but it is almost as if you were unclean and should have a bell round your neck to warn people of your approach.[118]

To his surprise, Cameron found that he received immense support from Christian feminists, to which he responded:

> Feminism is very much at the heretical end of the spectrum – understanding heresy of course in the praiseworthy sense of individual

---

[118] Peter Cameron, *Fundamentalism and Freedom*, Doubleday, Sydney, 1995, p. 57.

choice, nonconformism, adventure, innovation, creativity. And this is just what you expect from a new and radical movement, intent on establishing and promoting human rights and on questioning the traditional moulds and blinkered approaches of an uncritical and uncharitable establishment.[119]

The late Marie-Louise Uhr, founder of Ordination of Catholic Women (OCW), contended that, while 'desire for women's ordination continues to grow' in the Roman Catholic church, the main stumbling block is 'simply that the Pope has said it can't happen', and the Pope must be obeyed. She warned of the cost of continuing to defy the Vatican:

> So speaking out on this issue is a very dangerous thing to do, at least for anyone employed by the church or in any official position. And the hierarchy all around the world are silent... So, in some ways, I am buoyed up and believe that we can see real fruit from the last six or seven years of effort. At other times, it all seems like hitting our heads against the brick wall of Roman patriarchy. Yet for the members of OCW, the present papal 'no' is neither firmly founded on Scripture or Tradition, nor based on proper, widespread consultation with the whole church; moreover, it is harming relationships with other

---

[119] *Ibid.*, p. 32

Christian churches and with the wider world, and, above all, is causing deep hurt and great distress to the people of God.[120]

Undoubtedly, the Pope is still perceived as the most eminent Christian leader, and the Holy See, the Vatican, is treated as a political entity of a special kind. In his paper 'The Pope: Theory and Fact', Dr Eamon Duffy of Cambridge University explains that, from its inception, the papacy has been surrounded 'with a particular historical myth' that it was directly created by Jesus Christ in his lifetime, and that Christ wished his Church to be ruled by the apostles and their successors. Peter was considered to be the Supreme Apostle, the one with the most spiritual power, despite Peter's desertion of Christ when he was arrested and crucified.[121] This is certainly the belief which the Vatican is perpetuating in its Canon Law, suggesting that, as Peter's successor, the Pope's interaction with the Holy Spirit is more trustworthy and authoritative than the Spirit's interaction with the rest of Christendom.

Duffy refutes the claim that Jesus Christ instituted the papacy during his life on earth. Duffy considers that the historical evidence shows that Paul and Peter were both associated with the nascent Christian church in Rome. There were two shrines in Rome dedicated to Peter and Paul, established by Christians living in Rome during the early church period.

---

[120] Cited in *MOWatching*, Newsletter of Movement for the Ordination of Women (National) Inc., June 2000, p. 5.

[121] E. Duffy, 'The popes: theory and fact', *The Tablet*, 4 July 1998, pp. 871-873.

The Roman Church came into being about 40 CE, and for almost a century there was no supreme male bishop or pope. Nor were all the apostles associated with the establishment of the Roman Church male persons. In Romans 16:7, Paul acknowledged the work of Junia, who shared her ministry with Andronicus, and hailed her as 'foremost among the apostles'. This is an important historical and scriptural reality which is seldom mentioned because it might open to Roman Catholic women the door to priestly leadership. Junia and Andronicus travelled widely, teaching and preaching. In the fourth century, John Chrysostom spoke warmly about Junia the apostle, depicting her as a role model for Christian women,[122] a further indication that, in the early church women were playing senior leadership roles.

Duffy points out that everything we know about the Church at Rome in the first century or so indicates that it was in practice 'a loose and often divided federation of widely different communities'.[123] It was this disunity that led eventually to the emergence of the Roman episcopate. 'Thus, the emergence of the bishops of Rome was the result not straightforwardly of a direct and immediate act of the incarnate word of God in his own lifetime, but rather of a long and uncertain evolutionary process, which might conceivably have run a different way, which surely rules out any absolutist understanding of the nature of papal authority'. Jesus never set foot in Rome. The prominence of the Roman Church can be attributed to Emperor

---

[122] See Bernadette Brooten, 'Junia: Outstanding among the Apostles', in L. and A. Swidlers (ed.), *Women Priests*, Paulist Press, New York., 1992, pp. 35-40.
[123] *The Tablet*, 4 July 1998, p. 871.

Constantine's (272-337CE) adoption of Christianity as the state religion for the Roman Empire.

Duffy claimed that, from the beginning, the papacy 'has been resisted, and been rebuked by other Christian leaders'. In other words, historically it is not unusual for papal authority to be questioned. Duffy further pointed out that the papacy, after a period of decline, became more powerful after the French Revolution. He comments that 'the 1917 Code of Canon Law, which lies at the heart of papal domination of the modern Church, owed at least as much to the Napoleonic Code as to holy Scripture, and most of the actual exercise of papal authority in the modern Church is rooted in quite specific aspects of the institutional and intellectual history of the last two hundred years'.[124] Under the 1917 Code of Canon Law, popes were given the power to appoint directly the Catholic bishops of the world.

Duffy made clear the importance of understanding that the papacy can never remain a static, immutable body:

> It is because Catholics place so high a value on the papacy that we need constantly to remind ourselves that it is, like everything else in this world, a creature of time and circumstance. It has not always been so, it will change beyond our imaginings, and one day it will pass away.[125]

The siege mentality of the Vatican is understandable as it comes to grips with the rapidly changing perspectives and

---

[124] *Ibid.*, pp. 872-3.
[125] *Ibid.*, p. 873.

technologies which impinge upon it. Whether to reinforce old traditions and doctrines in the new millennium is debatable, but this is certainly the stratagem which is being adopted. Pope John Paul's apostolic letter was issued just prior to the opening of the historically important Lambeth Conference of 1998, at which eleven women bishops for the first time broke the male monopoly of the Anglican episcopate's decennial meeting. The Pope's insistence that the Roman Catholic priesthood must be male, and his reaffirmation of Pope Leo XIII's declaration of 1896 that Anglican orders were invalid, were clearly a rebuke to a Christian denomination which also claimed catholicity.

Pope John Paul, on 21 May 1998, when addressing a group of American bishops in Rome, maintained that churches which 'set sacramentality at the heart of the Christian life, and the Eucharist at the heart of sacramentality', were the Christian communities that 'don't believe they have the authority to ordain women'. He observed that 'Christian communities more readily confer a ministerial responsibility on women the further they move away from a sacramental understanding of the priesthood.'[126] This statement was inaccurate in that Anglicans and Old Catholics, both of which ordain women to priesthood, are deemed to be sacramental denominations in the apostolic succession tradition. Also, there are Anglican dioceses which refuse to ordain women to priesthood on the pretext that 'male headship' is an immutable doctrine, not because of a sacramental understanding of priesthood.

---

[126] Cited in *Ordination of Catholic Women News*, Vol. 5, No. 2, July 1998, p. 1.

Again, the not so subtle message to women is that their gender excludes them from entering the corridors of power.

The Vatican's denigration of churches which allow women to be ordained was followed by a further, more general statement which did not mention women at all. In September 2000, the Congregation for the Doctrine of the Faith issued a document *Dominus Iesus* (Lord Jesus) in which it was asserted that the uniqueness of Jesus Christ's salvific mediation is bound to the uniqueness of the Roman Catholic Church through apostolic succession and the Eucharist. While many salvific and ecclesial elements could be observed in other Christian denominations, the church which Christ founded existed in fullness in Roman Catholicism.

The document conceded that the Eastern Orthodox communities were closest to the acceptable standard because of their valid Eucharist and apostolic succession. Their imperfection was that they did not accept the authority of the Bishop of Rome. That the Orthodox Churches also strongly opposed the ordination of women was not mentioned in the document, but was, no doubt, a factor in their gaining papal favour.

According to Cardinal Ratzinger, in an official note dated 9 June 2000 addressed to the Roman Catholic bishops, 'the expression "sister churches" in the proper sense, as attested by the common tradition of East and West, may only be used for those ecclesial communities that have preserved a valid episcopate and Eucharist.[127]

---

[127] Cited in *Market-Place*, September 2000.

Not unexpectedly, many Christian denominations reacted to *Dominus Iesus* with astonishment. The document has been condemned as a setback for ecumenical dialogue. According to the then Archbishop of Canterbury, George Carey, 'the idea that Anglican and other churches are not "proper churches" seems to question the considerable ecumenical gains we have made'.[128] Even the English Roman Catholic paper, *The Tablet*, described *Dominus Iesus* as a 'public relations disaster' which sounded 'notes of triumphalism'. The Lutheran World Federation rejected the document because it reflected a different spirit from that encountered in Lutheran-Roman Catholic reconciliation discussions. Coincidentally, in the same month (September 2000) that *Dominus Iesus*, was proclaimed, the German Evangelical Lutheran Church elected Bärbel Wartenberg-Potter, a well-known female minister and ecumenist, as bishop of the Holstein-Lübeck diocese.

One of the issues in regard to ecumenical dialogue, which may currently be troubling Vatican conservatives, is the increasing interaction of its representatives with female bishops, priests and ministers. Roman Catholics are observing that women clergy are performing well and are widely accepted. This recognition gives credence to calls for theologically trained Catholic women to be ordained, at least to the diaconate, seeing that an increasing number of them are acting as pastoral assistants in parishes.

Despite threatening warnings issuing from the Vatican, a greater number of Catholic women are daring to speak out in defiance of papal directives on the issue of women's

---

[128] *Ibid*.

ordination. Marie-Louise Uhr queried whether the Catholic Church 'really sets the Eucharist at the heart of Christian life when it is prepared to deny most of its people access to regular Eucharists in order to uphold a male-only celibate priesthood as the only valid priesthood'.[129] Due to a chronic shortage of males training for priesthood, many Catholic parishes have had to miss out on full Eucharistic services because worship is led by nuns or lay people.

Uhr was disturbed that lay collaboration in ministry only arose out of expediency – a shortage of male priests. She drew attention to a Vatican document entitled 'The Instruction on Certain Questions Regarding the Collaboration of the Non-Ordained Faithful in the Sacred Ministry', commenting that 'the way the Curia's Instruction uses "sacred" to refer only to the ordained and never of the so-called lay faithful or non-ordained faithful would seem pertinent here'. She contrasted this with a passage from the theologian Karl Rahner's writings:

> Those who love, who are unselfish, who have a prophetic gift in the church, constitute the real church and are far from being always identical with the office-holders.[130]

Rahner's vision was for a 'de-clericalised church' in which the office-holders allow for the fact that 'the Spirit breathes where it will and that it has not arranged an exclusive and permanent tenancy with them'.[131]

---

[129] Cited in *Ordination of Catholic Women News*, Vol. 5, No. 2, July 1998, p. 1.
[130] *Ibid.*
[131] Cited in *Ordination of Catholic Women News*, April 1998, p. 1.

The Vatican's rejection of any sort of ordained ministry for women, including the diaconate, has for years been activating strong dissent. At the Third Dutch Ecumenical Women's Synod held in September 1997, the 300 participants called upon Pope John Paul II and the Congregation for the Doctrine of the Faith to reconsider their arguments concerning the ordination of women. Those present rejected the argument that the Roman Catholic Church lacks jurisdiction to ordain women to the priesthood. They claimed the dynamic core of the early church's faith was based in the confession that all who have been baptised in Christ have clothed themselves in Christ. Distinctions between male and female do not hold, according to Galatians 3:28.[132] The following statement was drawn up at the conclusion of the Synod:

> In the name of the Living One, we call upon the Bishop of Rome to leave the cul-de-sac which was entered when he ruled that the exclusion of women from ordained ministry belonged to the Tradition of Faith, and was to be held definitively by all the faithful.[133]

According to Sister Chris Schenk, a co-ordinator of the Catholic group 'A Call for National Dialogue on Women in Church Leadership', which is situated in the United States, 82% of 26,000 parish ministers are women, and perform similar functions to deacons. In 1994, a study carried out

---

[132] Cited in *Ibid.*, p. 9.
[133] *Ibid.*

by the Roman Catholic Canon Law Society of America found no canonical obstacles to opening the diaconate to women. Schenk contends that 'women's voices must be equally represented in church decision-making with those of men, or we will never be credible witnesses to Jesus Christ, who included women among his closest disciples.'[134]

In a Statement from the National Coalition of American Nuns in May 1995, it was disclosed that in seminaries women professors who spoke out against the Church authorities were experiencing job terminations and demotions:

> No matter how impressive their academic credentials, their teaching records, their publishing abilities, and their history of fidelity to the Church, there seems to be no room for women professors on seminary faculties. They have become a threat to the clericalism and triumphalism which too many seminarians today desire, profess and exemplify... In seeking a seminary which is doctrinally sound, many bishops find instead a factory of fear and a camp for exterminating deeper understandings.

In October 2002, an article by Christa Pongratz-Lippitt entitled 'A Priest called Ludmila' appeared in *The Tablet*. Ludmila Javorova was a woman priest, ordained in 1970 by Bishop Felix Davidek in the then underground Roman Catholic Church in Czechoslovakia. The bishop needed a woman priest to bring the sacraments to women in prison,

---

[134] *Ibid.*

including nuns, as women prisoners were not allowed to receive male visitors. Ludmila Javorova did not take services for other gatherings of Czechoslovakian Roman Catholics. When Czechoslovakia regained its independence in 1989, the Vatican refused to ratify Javorova's priesthood, despite the risks she had taken for the survival of the church under Communist rule.

The Vatican's decision on Ludmila Javorova further fuelled the resolve of Catholic women seeking ordination to press harder for reform. On 29 June 2002, seven Roman Catholic women were quietly ordained to priesthood at Passau, on the border between Austria and Germany. The ordination service took place aboard a boat on the Danube River, carried out by Bishop Dr Romulo Braschi, a leader of a splinter group called the 'Catholic-Apostolic Charismatic Church of Christ the King'. Braschi claimed to be a genuine Roman Catholic bishop since he was consecrated to the episcopate by Bishop Jeronimo Podesta of Avellaneda in Argentine. Podesta was relieved of his episcopal position in 1967 because he supported a married priesthood.

Of the seven women ordained, Dr Gisela Forster, Dr Ida Raming, Dr Iris Müller and Pia Brunner were from Germany and Christine Mayr-Lumetzberger, Sister Adelinde Theresia Roitinger and Angela Weiss (a pseudonym) were from Austria. The women were aware their ordinations would be problematic but believed their challenge to the Vatican was worth the risk involved. Their act of dissent was quickly followed by retributive action. On 5 August 2002, the

Congregation for the Doctrine of the Faith issued a decree of excommunication against the seven women.[135]

Two of the women priested at Passau, Christine Mayr-Lumetzberger and Gisela Forster, on 27 June 2003 announced that they had been made bishops in a private ceremony. The details have been kept secret to avoid punishment from the Vatican.[136] Women's ordinations have also been conducted in America in the Catholic Diocese of Rochester where the Corpus Christi parish split away and formed the Spiritus Christi Church. The ordinations were carried out by bishops independent of Rome, who belonged to another splinter church, the Ecumenical Communion of Catholic and Apostolic Churches. Although these ordinations are invalid in the eyes of the Vatican, they represent a grassroots refusal to accept the institutionalised bias against women in ministry.

The flow-on from constant reprisals against dissenters is that dynamism within the Church suffers and many of its most spiritually alive members are driven to find new ways to connect with God. The doctrinal stance of the veteran Christian denominations is being regarded as too narrow and politically outdated, too stereotyped and elitist to appeal to today's 'switched on' laity, and especially its youth.

A major problem in achieving reform is that Christian clergy have been taught to propagate only what is regarded as correct belief by their particular denomination. This code has been followed for centuries in Christian missions at home

---

[135] See J. Wijngaards, 'The Ordination of Catholic Women in Austria on the 29th of June 2002' on http://www.women priests.org/called/29jun02.htm

[136] See web site www.virtuelle-diozese.de

and abroad. Where Church and colonial power worked closely together, life could become difficult for indigenous peoples reluctant to change their belief systems. For many who resisted Christian evangelisation, the cost in terms of physical and mental suffering was high. For example, in Latin-America, dissent from Christianity could be life-threatening because it constituted a serious breach of white colonial law.

In Australia, the Christian churches have had to acknowledge that they tried to root out the beliefs of the indigenous peoples and replace them, not only with the faith beliefs of the West, but also with Western culture and English language. Today, there is growing recognition that there were traditions in Aboriginal belief systems which accorded well with the Christian gospels, such as respect for the environment. Ecotheology is increasingly being blended into Australian Christianity.

The Australian Aboriginal word *dadiri*, which means listening in silence in order to recognise the deep spring which lies within each person, accords remarkably well with Jesus' example of drawing apart for quiet meditation and prayer. According to Dr W. E. H. Stanner, who researched Australian belief systems, 'Aboriginal religion was probably one of the least material-minded and most life-minded of any of which we have knowledge'.[137]

---

[137] W. E. H. Stanner, 'On Aboriginal Religion', *Oceania Monograph* No. 11, cited in Patricia R. Dorrington, *The Serpent of Good and Evil: A Reconciliation in the Life and Art of Miriam-Rose Ungum err-Bauman*, Hyland House, Flemington, Vic., 2000, p. 114.

Love has always been at the centre of Christ's message – love for God and love for the people one encounters in daily living, irrespective of sex, race or class. The problem for Christianity, especially in denominations where power and authority are invested in an exclusive hierarchy, is that the love at the heart of Jesus Christ's gospel is given less priority than adherence to canon law, tradition and clergy collegiality. This situation is even more untenable when one discovers that canon law and tradition were inherently biased and flawed from the time of their institutionalisation in that they discriminated against at least one half of humanity.

Christian institutions need to reclaim and prioritise the message of love for all people in their practices and liturgy, so that love becomes a focal point rather than a vague, abstract ideal. Restructuring on the basis of love and understanding would enable church leaders to handle more sensitively and rationally the challenges raised by dissenters. A more balanced approach to gender might draw people back to the church, and so stem the present exodus.

In the past, in western society, moving away from mainstream Christianity was regarded as aberrant, especially if the shift entailed a rejection of approved concepts about God. Lina O'Leary, in her article 'Apostasy: Exploring Resistance and Transformation', sees the trend today as 'one of transition', pointing to Michel Foucault's analyses of the power relations or techniques of power which constrain modern individuals:

> Whether apostasy is a response to secularisation
> in a modern world, which leaves individuals

without faith, or whether it is a system of modernity's construction of religion, may be dependent upon the individual's relationship to a post-modern world... Truth and power conspire to create an indivisible reality for the individual which can be highly constraining. This is particularly true when the 'religious' is embedded within power relations.[138]

According to Foucault, 'a system of constraint becomes truly intolerable when the individuals who are affected by it don't have the means for modifying it. This can happen when such a system becomes intangible as a result of its being considered a moral or religious imperative.'[139] Foucault concedes that one can always resist such domination, though the cost may be high in terms of loss of faith.

O'Leary argues that studies of 'apostasy' can be used to explore post-modernity and the impact which this new form of society has on the constitution of the post-modern subject. She states:

> Apostasy under these circumstances can now be explored as representative of new epistemological approaches to knowledge, no longer a process of resistance, but perhaps

---

[138] Lina O'Leary, 'Apostasy: Exploring Resistance and Transformation', *Australian Religious Studies Review*, Vol. 13, No. 1, Autumn, 2000, p. 22. Apostasy is a total desertion, or departure from, one's religion.

[139] M. Foucault, *Power/Knowledge, Selected Interviews and Other Writings*, 1972-1977, Harvester Press, London, 1980, p. 21.

processes of reflection and transformation of the self, now possible in post-modernity.[140]

Religious nonconformity is not only acceptable in the twenty-first century, it is becoming a social norm. Many of the institutions on which Church traditions were built are decaying, highlighting the need for new 'living traditions'. People often ask, why don't the churches just throw out all that outdated stuff and start all over again, retaining just the relevant essentials? They fail to recognise how legally enmeshed church systems have become. Christian denominations have so thoroughly canonised their scriptures, beliefs and traditional systems that massive unravelling processes would need to take place to legitimise change – almost beyond the powers of bishops and synods. In these circumstances, the formation of new religious communities appears the easiest pathway to renewal and transformation. The cost is that Christ's church becomes even more fragmented.

Monica Furlong, the late English Anglican writer and broadcaster, observed that strategies for renewal in her church tended to centre around efficiency and better management – 'bums on seats programmes'. Changes appeared little more than diversionary tactics, 'a palliative drug, a Prozac that leaves the underlying problems untouched, when what is needed is to look much more profoundly and honestly into the reasons for the decline, and to recognise that, whatever the role of the Church in the

---

[140] L. O'Leary, 'Apostasy', p. 25.

future, the chances are that it will be quite different from the past'.[141]

There are today a few encouraging signs of efforts to change the outdated system. For example, recently retired Archbishop Peter Carnley of Perth has been referred to as 'God's guerrilla' because his views on the resurrection and on multifaith dialogue were regarded by conservative Anglicans as verging on the heretical.[142] Carnley admitted that his biggest challenge has been to make the church more relevant to the majority of Australians 'who do not line the pews':

> I was called to do this... to keep the church together. Harmonious, peaceful but also maintained in truth. My main task was to foster conversation in a harmonious, civilised and courteous way, but if people want to step outside of that ball-game, then there may have to be a bit of a skirmish to establish where truth lies.[143]

Today, church leaders are limited in what they can do to handle dissenters. They may not use any means which would constitute a crime in secular society, for they would be answerable to the civil courts if they were deemed to have acted unlawfully. Yet a religious reproof which is not secularly unlawful can still be psychologically and economically very painful. For many Christians, alienation

---

[141] Monica Furlong, 'Are the laity now seen as too big for their boots?', in *Church Times*, 4 February 2000.
[142] See *Weekend Australian*, 29-30 April 2000.
[143] *Ibid.*

from their church can cause concern. Defiance of church rulings may raise the fear of being listed in God's black books. To some Christians, the threat of hell and damnation remains a frightening possibility.

Religious socialisation which suggests that bliss in the next world depends on virtuous behaviour in one's mortal life, can stifle the urge to resist oppressive religious structures. Obedience and unquestioning faith was for centuries the price a Christian, and especially a woman, was expected to pay to ensure a trouble-free, serene spiritual afterlife. Bishop John Spong has commented on this situation:

> Justice was God's business and would be attended to in the Kingdom of Heaven, where it was an unquestioned article of faith that the good would be rewarded and the evil punished. That promise removed any necessity for reform movements... People were taught to accept and to live within the status into which they had been born...[144]

The concept of Heaven is much less clearly defined now than in the past, more an abstract concept than God's extended mansion in the sky. Similarly, the concept of Hell has lost credence, regarded at worst as a period of alienation from God rather than a place of burning fires and eternal torture. Eternal life is being more and more regarded among

---

[144] J. S. Spong, *Why Christianity must Change or Die*, p. 202.

non-fundamentalist Christians as a spiritual afterlife where one attains a closer association with God.

There are still mainstream churchgoers, especially the elderly, who support the *status quo* and dislike modernisation. The traditions, rituals and denominational loyalties which are associated with Christian worship, become deeply rooted in people's lives. They are not easily discarded. Any decision to disaffiliate from one's church is seldom taken lightly. Dissent becomes more painful when love of old forms of worship and the search for truth draw a person in two opposite directions. This dilemma has been articulated by a Roman Catholic parishioner in her article 'Altarpiece':

> The church encompasses not only what I most love but also what I feel most wounded by. It is authoritarian, dogmatic, male supremacist and exclusive. The liturgy includes readings from the Old Testament which can sanction, in the sacred content of the Mass, xenophobia, religious intolerance, deep misogyny and endemic violence. I have come to see this paradigm as underpinning not just the Catholic Church but Christianity as a whole, and hence the spirituality and culture of Western civilisation.[145]

Worshipping in a situation of old traditions and new realities is not a situation conducive to spiritual serenity. The twentieth century produced major shifts away

---

[145] Anna March, 'Altarpiece' in *Women/Church*, No. 26, Autumn, 2000, p. 19.

from traditional conceptualisations, such as the feminist movement, anti-colonialism/anti-racism, the ecological movement, and advanced knowledge of the nature of the universe. These major shifts challenged accepted theological beliefs, and began to edge out the concept of a monarchical, omniscient deity, who controlled everything from his heavenly residence in the sky.

The major contribution of the feminist movement, as we have seen, was to challenge the male-only pinnacles of power which exist in most religious and secular institutions. Women have shown considerable courage in taking a strong stand against discrimination in the face of threats and warnings from their religious leaders. They have learned to ignore the hierarchical put-downs and accusations of being heretical, self-promoting and immodest. The advantage for women in their campaigns is the knowledge that their presence is essential to the viability of the churches, as the historical record has shown.

Christian churches are slowly changing male traditions in response to the protests of women, though at an insufficient rate to attract new generations of women back to the pews. Female embodiment is increasingly present in church sanctuaries, so long the preserve of males. But as the voices calling for reform intensify, the old men in the Vatican become more defensive. Similarly, in the Orthodox Churches, women are finding it difficult to achieve female embodiment of priesthood.

7

The Importance of Gender Balance in Belief Systems

The nascent twenty-first century has already experienced the rapid development of new technologies. Sophisticated communication devices have proliferated, many beneficial but some harmful, such as remote-control detonators of destructive devices, computer viruses and internet crime scams. Men and women from a range of cultures and religions are interacting with one another across the world as never before, not just at elite levels but increasingly at the grassroots.

For Christians, these new technologies provide opportunities for freer exchange of viewpoints than in the past. These exchanges do not just take place locally but across denominational and faith barriers involving a wider range of people, in a milieu free from clergy disapproval and condemnation. Decrees and statements issued by popes, archbishops and patriarchs can be critiqued on-line in bolder language than that normally used in church circles, without fear of retribution. For churchwomen dissatisfied with their unequal status in the church, these new channels of communication have been a blessing, providing new ways to link with and support other women who are likewise disenchanted.

Sociological research and census figures indicate that Christianity is in decline in its European heartland, though not in North America. Christianity is presently vibrant in Africa, parts of Asia, the Pacific islands and South America, perhaps because Christian relief and educational agencies established close bonds with grassroots people in those regions. In Australia, Christianity started badly in 1788, being regarded more as a social controller for an unruly penal colony than as an institution dispensing love and compassion. In the late nineteenth and early twentieth centuries, mainstream Christianity of varying denominations flourished, but never integrated into the developing social culture as strongly as in other British colonies. Today, in Australia, Christian decline is certainly the prevailing pattern.

According to the Roman Catholic Archbishop of Brisbane, John Bathersby, 'we have about 600,000 nominal Catholics in the archdiocese', but he admits that 'only 13 per cent of these are worshippers who would be there every Sunday... Attendance by those under 18 has dropped right down to single figures'.[146] Most Anglican churches in Australia also report declining numbers although Anglicanism was once the largest denomination. The

---

[146] Cited in *Courier Mail*, 31 July 2004.

Pentecostal Christian churches are those noticeably growing in popularity in Australia, but still represent a small section of the population.

The growth of fundamentalism in all major faiths is a worrying trend, perceived to be a defensive reaction to uncertainties about basic beliefs created by modernisation and new scientific discoveries. Fundamentalists seek a stable, infallible version of their faith, which they hope will be immune to the influences of advances in knowledge and differing world views. They prefer to believe that God remains in full control and is omnipresent. Fundamentalists insist that their ancient scriptures are historically accurate rather than allegorical and to some extent mythical. They show a dislike for pluralism, relativism, and liberalism. Another worrying trend in fundamentalism is its militant judgmental piety and its desire to contain its adherents within a strictly controlled religious environment. Male headship tends to prevail.

For those areas where Christianity is in decline, the immediate challenge is how to remain a significant social force, relevant to 21st century people, especially youth. Restructuring of basic tenets and church practices would appear to be the logical remedial action to take. The problem is, how does one regenerate a religious system which is so closely tied to ancient texts written in cultural forms which are thousands of years old? Can Christianity be regenerated by providing more relevant 'scriptures' for this new century, retaining the Bible as a revered reference book?

Essentially, the Old Testament provides valuable insights into how Jewish perceptions of God evolved, while the New Testament records the radical part Jesus Christ played in trying to reform the Jewish belief system. In future restructuring of Christianity, it will be important to downplay or remove those sections of scripture which are steeped in tribal misogyny and divine avenging militancy. More emphasis should be given to Jesus Christ's assertion that God loves all people, regardless of gender, race and status, and seeks justice and peace rather than war.

Jesus Christ, despite the patriarchal Middle Eastern culture in which he lived on Earth, provided a positive role model which has validity for today. Jesus' concern for others, his rejection of exploitation of the weaker members of society, his willingness to include women in his movement and his bravery in facing death on a cross to advance God's kingdom on earth, has relevance for all generations. His 'code of ethics' was revolutionary in the first century and is still counter-cultural in terms of today's global society.

A God who epitomises the values of love, peace and justice is certainly relevant, with our planet reeling under conflict and pandemics erupting on its continents, with violent and rapacious rulers riding roughshod over their subjects, denying them basic rights and robbing them of their nation's economic wealth. The extent of poverty which exists in the world is not abating, despite the Millennium goals to address this important issue. If today's Christian leaders are genuine about emulating the God proclaimed by Jesus Christ, then it is important that they examine their existing institutions to ensure that they meet the standards set by Jesus. If the ecclesiology of any Christian denomination has serious flaws and discrimination built into its basic tenets, then today's discerning critics will claim that the Christian faith is failing in its duty to be a light to all people.

While sociological research into religion confirms that a considerable number of people today still believe in God, it seems that many find it more difficult to accept that God is the creator and controller of all that happens in this world, or other worlds in the universe. God is gradually being divested of responsibility for all that was and is and of all that occurs. With notable exceptions, God is not now regarded as the instigator or supporter of military action. There is a growing perception of God as a spiritual force for good, who prioritises love for all creation, who is not vindictive about human failings, and who has a broader perspective on 'sin' and its underlying causes than the God of tradition. This is not an eclectic, 'new age' approach. This empathetic God can be found in many parts of the scriptures, including the Old Testament, but has not been accorded sufficient doctrinal and liturgical weight in Christianity over the centuries.

Any adequate understanding of what science has to say and what it is inherently unable to explain, allows for an 'ecological' concept of nature and the universe, in which purpose can operate. Such an ecological world view also allows for the possibility, or even the necessity, of a continual involvement of God's creative activity in the universe. God is then understood as the 'ground of being', the ground of order and novelty, intimately involved in cosmic evolution. God's involvement in cosmic evolution could include the evolution of life as we know it, and possibly of life as we do not understand it.

The ecological or organic model of the universe includes recognition of the necessary role of chance in the evolution of the cosmos and the concomitant requirement that chance allows the possibility of disorder and evil. A world without chance would be a world without any possibility of freedom, spontaneity, and purpose. As the late Australian scientist, Charles Birch, has commented on the prevailing concept of an all-powerful controller of the universe, 'for God to completely control the world would be the same as to annihilate it'.[147] God is not then the all powerful, all manipulating and omnipotent ruler of the universe. God is instead perceived as acting through persuasive love, as in the biblical image of one who stands at the door and knocks, presenting the opportunity for response.

Any transformation of the traditional God in the sky to a deity perceived as an indwelling spiritual force will no doubt cause angst among many traditional Christians. People worry about their own after life; they feel more assured by belief in an ongoing existence in a delightful sanctuary named Heaven. Christians have gained solace from the thought of a blessed everlasting existence, surrounded by their deceased loved ones, in close communion with God and Jesus. The problem is that, with increasing knowledge about space and the vastness of the universe, it is becoming more difficult to accept ancient religious views about Heaven. The positive factor is that the new focus on the indwelling God actually experienced by most Christians, *does not* cancel out the possibility of a continuing spiritual relationship with God when earthly life ends. Afterlife remains part of the great unknown.

Women today seek a theology which is gender-balanced to overcome the prevailing bias that divinity must be totally

---

[147] Charles Birch, *On Purpose*, New South Wales University Press, Kensington, NSW, 1991, p. 73.

male to be supreme and glorious. As noted previously, women globally are living daily in situations of suffering and abuse because of gender imbalance. The number of women being sold into sexual slavery is escalating. Women desperately need to have their status upgraded and sanctified. Yet the leaders of the two major denominations in the Christian faith, Roman Catholicism and Orthodoxy, fail to take male bias seriously. Church leaders in the senior mainstream churches are so enmeshed in their sacred male traditions that they are not fulfilling their duties of care to all people. While churchmen continue to denigrate women, denying them their true religious worth, they fail to represent Jesus Christ faithfully. As more women become aware of this unfair, un-Christlike behaviour, churches will continue to lose the faithful female members on whom they have depended so much since Christianity was founded.

The exclusion of women from high office not only damages Christianity but creates a distorted pattern of how society should be structured. In 2009, warfare and acts of terrorism keep erupting around the world, instigated predominantly by male aggressors, many using religion to fuel their cause. Women have inadequate influence in the dynamics of global conflict since so few females are allowed to become either political or religious leaders. Yet every day, women and children become victims of warfare and male abuse in general. Amnesty International reports that there is 'an ongoing cycle of violence against women', claiming that 'crimes against women are all a product of a global culture that continues to discriminate against women, denying them equal rights and equal opportunities'.[148] The tragic reality is that, while mainstream Christian leaders continue to deny equal status to churchwomen, they are providing the wrong paradigm for the secular world to follow.

Now is the time for self-examination by Christian church leaders to perceive whether upholding the doctrine of male supremacy in theology, ecclesiology and general practice is the correct model for a world torn apart by religiously inspired male aggression. Any attempt to change the existing male culture must express fullness of life for all people, - and must also resonate with the needs of those living in the 21st century. Liturgies, doctrines and general church discourse need the input of female symbolism, to counter the existing presumption that God is an omnipotent male. Images of God as a nurturer of life rather than a militant monarch might dispel misconceptions that God would ever be a supporter of warfare.

Clearly, the achievement of a gender-balanced religious culture will entail laborious procedures, certain to encounter considerable resistance from those who cherish the old patriarchal system. From the preceding chapters, we have observed that the mainstream Christian denominations have developed into institutions resistant to major change. While clergy and parishioners at the grassroots are the ones most alarmed by declining numbers in the pews, resulting in shrinking finances and a scarcity of young parishioners, they do not have the power to take major remedial action. Because old beliefs, dogmas and traditions are legally set in stone,

---

[148] See Amnesty International, *The Human Rights Defender*, Vol. 23, No. 2, April, 2004, p. 7.

parish leaders are afraid to act too radically in case such action draws rebuke from those in the upper echelons of the church.

Even bishops and top-level clergy who privately acknowledge that women's demand for reform is just, are reluctant to speak out too vociferously on their behalf. Most clergy have been insufficiently encouraged in their seminary training to analyse critically the basic doctrines of the religious system in which they will hold office. The emphasis in clergy commissioning has been to defend their faith from dissenters, and to maintain orthodoxy. Senior clergy have dedicated their life to their church system, have risen through the ranks in it and have been prepared to accept limited economic rewards for its sake. For clergy, the sacred aura which surrounds those in ordained ministry, the feeling that they are closest to God, is probably the most satisfying element in their lives. When confronted with suggestions that their esteemed system is redundant, they instinctively close ranks to protect it.

An effective method of gaining a deeper understanding of the underlying problems in mainstream Christianity would be for church leaders to include on advisory committees concerned with renewal, a balanced proportion of church members who are dissatisfied with the status quo. This type of action is seldom taken, seen as being too threatening. Church leaders also need to liaise with former church members, especially youth and women, to hear directly their reasons for dropping out. Interaction with the 'lost sheep' will certainly bring to the surface many disturbing issues, which senior clergy and conservative laity may be reluctant to tackle for fear of exceeding the boundaries of what is acceptable. But if leaders want Christianity to survive, the perspective of the disillusioned Christian will need to be taken seriously.

It is interesting to observe how mainstream churches are addressing the loss of young people once they reach their teens. In the Church of England, for example, it has been 'recognised that other forms of Christian community are needed beyond the familiar parish framework, not to replace it but to augment or supplement it' such as 'network, cafe and cell churches'.[149] These forms of assembly, being informal, are more likely to be gender-balanced. Interestingly, in all the proposals put forward to enhance church numbers, there is seldom mention of scripting a church liturgy that is gender-balanced in every respect.

Patriarchal forms of Christianity thrived while churches had the support of state authority, the downside being the compromise of the egalitarian ethos set within the first century Jesus movement. When Church and State worked in tandem, Jesus' command to spread his vision of God around the world was deliberately distorted to suit national interests. Too often Christian conversion was associated with economic and political exploitation, thus undermining the major commandments established by Jesus, that is, love and respect for God and all people, irrespective of race, gender, or status. The freedom to search out truths, so much encouraged by Jesus, was compromised by the introduction of rigid doctrinal control.

The Rev. Dr George Tinker, a Native American Indian scholar, has commented on how the combination of colonial

---

[149] Cited in *Market-Place*, July 2004.

expansion and Western missionary endeavour affected his people:

> The illusion of Western world superiority has functioned implicitly, and at times brutally, explicitly to facilitate the conquest and enslavement of native peoples... The religious institutions of the 'West' have consistently lent legitimacy to those acts. At some level, the church has ultimately functioned to provide theological justification for acts of conquest, even when it has protested to the contrary or interceded at the surface level on behalf of the conquered.[150]

Dr Anne Pattel-Gray, an Australian Aboriginal sociologist, who has written prolifically on racism, comments that her people want a form of Christianity which is free from elements of Western domination. She states that 'an Aboriginal Christian community may have been happy in the past to live with a hybrid culture but today, the challenge is to become fully Aboriginal through inculturation of Christ into our midst'.[151]

For many Christians today, key doctrines, shaped by ancient religious practices, appear inappropriate for this age. Queries are being raised by Christian scholars whether Jesus' crucifixion at the hands of the Roman imperialist regime

---

[150] George E. Tinker, *Missionary Conquest: The Gospel and Native American Cultural Genocide*, Fortress Press, Minneapolis, 1993, pp. vi-vii.

[151] Anne Pattel-Grey, 'The Aboriginal Process of Inculturation', 2003 Penny Magee Lecture, in *Australian Religion Studies Review*, Vol. 17, No. 1, Autumn, 2004, p. 14.

should have been interpreted as the human sacrifice God required to redeem all people from their sins. The days of belief in blood sacrifice to appease deities are past. Blood sacrifice is now generally regarded as a primitive, even barbaric, religious response.

A more positive approach to the crucifixion would be to view it as a supreme act of courageous integrity and fearless defence of the values of the domain of God. Jesus was determined to spread abroad a life-affirming image of God, a gospel of unconditional love, justice and respect for other people. He died because his message was unacceptable to the colonial rulers and the religious leaders of his day.

Scripture writers and early theologians linked Jesus' crucifixion to the Creation myth in Genesis, where Adam and Eve fell from grace and were expelled from the Garden of Eden for their sinfulness in not obeying God's command. They argued that, through the sacrificial death of his son, God would restore humankind to the state of goodness which it possessed when first created. This doctrine of Original Sin is presently under scrutiny, regarded as incompatible with what is known about Jesus. As females for centuries have been deemed to be innately sinful because of Eve's fall from grace, the revision of this ancient theology could only be beneficial for women.

Jesus' attitudes towards women were enlightened for his times. Jesus never suggested that women were 'fallen' like Eve, and therefore deserved to suffer and remain in a situation of eternal subordination to men. Jesus encouraged women to speak out and spread his gospel. First century women dared to cross cultural divides to follow Jesus, probably because he encouraged all around him to make use of their talents, irrespective of gender. Although the Christian scriptures will always present a problem for women because they focus so much on the deeds and utterances of males, the New Testament writers could not in honesty conceal the reality that, in the early church, women played extraordinarily brave and self-sacrificial pastoral roles, despite the dangers they faced, not only by breaching the norms in their society, but by being members of a recusant religious group. They set an example for today's churchwomen to follow.

Jesus, Christians believe, reflected the true nature of God, therefore the actions and attitudes of Jesus are seen as closest to the reality of God. Jesus did not confine his socialisation to Jewish people, nor did he mainly fraternise with religious teachers and Jewish leaders. He had no qualms about developing deep relationships with those categorised as 'sinners' or 'religiously polluting'. Outreach to people on the margins was a notable phenomenon of his ministry. Jesus' emphasis on ministry to the weak, the oppressed, and the socially undesirable has been given less priority since Christianity was adopted as a religion of the State. Church leaders were expected to be moral watchdogs, teaching their flocks to be law-abiding citizens. Church members were led to believe that God sanctioned the close ties between State and Church. Women, as we have seen, were treated as second-class human beings in both Church and State, deemed to be of lesser spiritual worth because of their innately weak and sinful nature. Claiming God on their side was a potent weapon for patriarchs.

People were taught to communicate with God as dependent children and miserable sinners. Bishop John

Spong has been critical of this approach and feels that it needs to be changed:

> I am free of the God who was deemed to be incomplete unless constantly receiving our endless praises, the God who required that we acknowledge ourselves as born in sin and therefore as helpless; the God who seemed to delight in punishing sinners, the God, who, we were told, gloried in our childlike grovelling dependency.[152]

The term 'Father' is the one most commonly used for God in Christianity because it was how the human man Jesus addressed God in the Gospel stories. In the first century, Jewish fathers had legal power and authority, while wives were dependants, so it would have been culturally difficult for Jesus to use the term 'Mother' as a metaphor for God. In the 21st century, the dominant father figure of the past is giving way to the reality of varied familial relationships. Women today are often sole parents, and natural fathers are being replaced in the home by male partners/stepfathers. The need today is to find a metaphor for God which is neither familial nor gender-biased.

Josephine Griffith comments on the unsuitability of 'Father' as a way of addressing God in her work *Seeking Sophia*:

---

[152] . S. Spong, *A New Christianity for a New World*, HarperCollins, New York, 2001, p. 75.

> Fatherhood for a great many human beings does not carry connotations of love and benign authority. 'Dad' is not always the highest and best experience of caring that a person has... For some people 'mother' is nearer in experience to the caring authority you are expressing; but for many parenthood is not a useful model at all.[153]

A non-parental way of envisioning God will entail a re-conception of the Trinity. Changes are already taking place in some churches, with the use of terminology such as 'God – Creator, Redeemer and Sanctifier' to express the trinitarian form of Godhead. Re-imaging will compensate for the damage which has been done to women by portraying the trinitarian Godhead as totally male. The Holy Spirit, the Wisdom of God, lost its usual feminine term Sophia as the early Christian theologians instituted the term Logos, the Divine Word, a male gender term.

Jesus' teachings about caring for the underprivileged and relieving the burdens of the poorest of the poor are certainly relevant in today's world. Jesus' warnings to the rich to accept their responsibility to assist people less fortunate than themselves are also timely. It is in giving aid to and serving the disadvantaged at the grassroots level, that churches are perhaps most Christlike today, as long as their service is as free as possible from cultural imperialism. To their credit, church leaders are constantly drawing attention to the extent of economic injustice which exists in the world today. But as mainstream Christianity declines, so

---

[153] J. Griffiths, *Seeking Sophia*, p. 45.

the Christian voice becomes only one among the appeals made by humanitarian aid agencies. Nor have Christian leaders emphasised sufficiently that the people most at risk in poverty-stricken societies are females – wives and daughters.

The persisting assumption that a deity with female characteristics would pertain to paganism has been a major factor in the continued exaltation of masculinity in Christianity. Few Christians are aware that divinity was not always portrayed as masculine in Hebrew scripture. Before Hebrew religion became monotheistic, there were goddesses as well as gods, some beneficial and life-giving, others spiteful and aggressive. When the concept of one God was instituted, the feminine side of deity was played down, and God was predominantly written into Scripture as a male.

As the early Christian communities slowly replaced the ancient pagan religions of Europe, their leaders became aware that newly converted pagans were reluctant to relinquish mother goddess figures such as Artemis. The elevation of the Virgin Mary to be the Queen of Heaven helped to provide a substitute for the goddesses which had been so loved by the pagans. Yet, although named Queen of Heaven, Mary was never deified; she remained outside the Trinity. Especially in Roman Catholicism, Mary became perceived as biologically unique, eternally maiden, whose baby Jesus did not rupture her hymen in the process of childbirth.

Yet, as we have discussed, for several centuries Mary was also regarded as a priest, until the Vatican in the early twentieth century deemed that this was no longer an appropriate role for her. The early twentieth century was the time when Christian women began to seek ordination in the Protestant denominations. The Virgin Mary from then on was used to emphasise that motherhood and attention to family duties were the most Godly roles for Christian females. If they chose to remain single, then women were encouraged to enter a convent.

In the 21st century, women world-wide are establishing defence systems against male hegemony. Women taking up senior positions in the secular workforce increasingly expect to be treated like anyone else in their profession. Any religion which institutes male gender as a criterion for senior leadership must expect to lose many of its most capable female members. Women who choose to remain in the church are trying to circumnavigate the gender biases they encounter by strongly voicing their protests. As Gillian Paterson, a campaigner against sexual discrimination, reminds women, 'We have left the safety of the ranks, but we are aliens still in the corridors of power.'[154]

So, what reforms are essential for improving relationships between men and women in the future Church? One of the first and seemingly simplest steps to take would be for the Vatican and Orthodox Patriarchates, the major players, to amend the discriminatory canons and edicts which exclude women and married men from top leadership, and laity generally from major decision-making roles. Once women are affirmed as being spiritually equal to men in all areas of the church, and biologically as acceptable to God, the male-dominant structures would lose validity. A partnership of equals would counteract the existing gender

---

[154] Gillian Paterson, *Still Flowing*, p. 115.

imbalance and make Christianity a much healthier and spiritually fulfilling environment for worshippers.

Jan Punch, a former Roman Catholic, acknowledges her frustration with the church because of its refusal to listen to the voices of women. She views the Vatican's method of dealing with pressures to reform as adjusting the system 'to maintain, not to make major change'. To Jan Punch, the term 'church' now only represents a building:

> Instead of saying 'we are Church'... I prefer to declare that we are Christ, which is none of the Vatican's business. The Vatican is a men's club. It has proclaimed women off limits... I will not acquiesce in the Vatican's misogyny for to do so is to participate in the crucifixion.

According to Punch, people have the alternative of keeping the Vatican's ego afloat with their mental support or of detaching. 'Let it sink and know that Jesus is supplying lifeboats'.[155]

The greatest incentive for remedial action in Christianity is the reality of empty pews. Older churchwomen, who have been involved most of their lives in the maintenance of their churches, are especially conscious that the children they took so regularly to church, Sunday school and youth groups, have ceased attending in adulthood. They notice that, although elderly, their generation is bearing much of the parish workload. The loss of younger Christians is so noticeable that when youth venture into churches, they feel

---

[155] Jan Punch, 'Loyal Dissent' in *Women-Church*, No. 27, Spring 2000, p. 20.

alienated. As my granddaughter Stephanie, aged 7 years, whispered to me one Easter Sunday when I took her to the morning service: 'Is church a place for Grannies and Grandpas?'

Education has played a major role in breaking down the barriers which have kept women subordinate. As more women advance to higher posts in professional and political fields, gender-balance is less viewed as a feminist ploy, becoming a value in itself. Response to calls for gender-balance in the past tended to be limited to the inclusion of one 'token' woman on committees. Today, women are increasingly being accepted as associates of powerful males. But viewed universally rather than from the Western perspective, progress for women is slower. Globally, men hold 91% of the best and most important jobs. Women still do the bulk of the household management and childcare.

In countries where women are advancing in the public workplace, churches are still lagging behind. Roman Catholicism and Eastern Orthodoxy are so strongly based on structures of patriarchal authority that more gender-balanced ways of being Christian are regarded as heretical. Tradition has been lionised to such divine heights that it has become almost immutable. For example, the response from Archbishop Stylianos, a leader of the Australian Orthodox communities, to calls for change was to blame the secular world. 'We see modern man being more sceptical and unbelieving than the previous generations of faithful precisely because our times uphold an almost allergic antipathy towards every notion of institutional power and authority.'[156]

Pressures for an overhaul of archaic church systems keep mounting, with reform initiatives taking place at the grassroots levels. For example, I have before me a document entitled 'A Proposed Constitution of the Catholic Church' published by the Association for the Rights of Catholics in the Church, a group based in New Jersey, USA. This proposed constitution was drafted in conjunction with Catholic colleagues in Europe. The writers explain that the document is not written in theological language or in terms of ecclesiology because its focus is on 'governance'. The writers offer the following comment in explanation:

> It [the proposed constitution] has been drawn up from the pastoral perspective, recognising that the principal level or forum of Christian life takes place at community or parish level and... it is at that local level that most of the decision-making should take place... The Constitution is radically different from the pyramid model, which in the church has evolved over the centuries, resulting with the Pope and Vatican at the pinnacle, the laity at the bottom, and with the priests, bishops and religious orders somewhere in between.[157]

---

[156] Cited in "'The Lamb' and 'The Bridegroom'", in *The Voice of Orthodoxy*, Vol. 19, No. 5, June 1998, p. 49.

[157] *A Proposed Constitution of the Catholic Church*, The Association for the Rights of Catholics in the Church, P. O. Box 902, Delran, New Jersey, n.d.

Among basic rights laid down in the document was the right of Catholics to 'follow their informed conscience in all matters'. The 'right to express publicly in a responsible manner their agreement or disagreement regarding decisions made by Church authorities' was also stated. These declarations are clearly a rebuttal of the Vatican's tendency to excommunicate dissident scholars and to ban debate on subjects of which it disapproves.

The document also claimed the right of Catholics, whether laity or clergy, to marry or remain single, to divorce and remarry, to determine the size of their families and to choose appropriate methods of contraception. There was also a strong statement that Catholic women should have an equal right with men to the resources and exercise of all the powers of the Church. This statement, if ever adopted, would licence a woman to become a Pope, although attention was not drawn to this fact in the document. Of course, being a Pope in a democratic system would not be the same as in the present papal power structure.

In Section D on 'Leaders', it was declared, under subsection 3, that 'all commissioned officeholders of ministries shall be chosen in a manner which shall give a representative voice to all those who are to be led by them'. 'This is especially true of the local pastor, the Diocesan bishop and the Pope'.[158] The Pope shall be elected for a single ten-year term by delegates selected by National Councils.

This 'Proposed Constitution' has been designed to democratise the Catholic Church right through to the apex of power. It is also interesting that the term 'priest' is replaced

---

[158] *Ibid.*, p. 8.

by 'pastor', indicating that the pastoral role of the parish leader is of as great significance as his/her administration of the Eucharist. The term 'Pastor' does not require the use of the parental term 'Father'. The document emphasised that 'through Baptism everyone has a common membership, therefore status cannot be accorded because of a specific role, vocation or commissioning. There are no classes of membership.'

Documents like the 'Proposed Constitution', coming from a Catholic group on the eve of the new millennium, indicate that drastic reform is recognised to be a major issue in future Catholicism. The key changes which are being sought are the decentralisation of power and authority, the cancellation of the celibacy requirement for clergy and the removal of exclusion of women from any office on the grounds of gender. Clause (a) in Section B of the document, which states that 'all Catholic women have an equal right with men to the resources and the exercise of all the powers of the Church', is a particularly liberating one for those Catholic women who are presently exercising 'priestly' ministry, but who can only be categorised as 'pastoral assistants'.

This document reveals the deep resentment many Roman Catholics feel because of their inability to bypass the Vatican to legalise change. However, in 2010, there is still a yawning chasm between the present reality and the aspirations of progressive Catholics. Many Catholics, though sympathetic to the views expressed by the progressive wing, would claim that it was wishful thinking that such long-institutionalised layers of domination (and for some oppression) could be removed in the twenty-first century. The progressives may be in a category which Josephine Griffith refers to as the 'goats buzzing around an elephant'.[159]

There are senior members of the Roman Catholic Church who are listening to what grassroots members of the church are saying. At the October 1999 synod of European bishops, Cardinal Carlo Maria Martini, Archbishop of Milan, presented a new vision for Roman Catholicism. Because of the Church's inability to recruit significant candidates for priesthood, he advocated that priestly celibacy should be re-examined, claiming it had never been a basic Catholic teaching. Martini also urged his fellow bishops to reconsider the Vatican's position on the role of women and on the subject of sexuality *per se*. Martini, in a radio broadcast in November 1999, also questioned the doctrine of papal supremacy, suggesting a more decentralised structure, allowing local bishops to make decisions on moral and pastoral questions without the acquiescence of the Vatican. Martini was favoured to succeed Pope John Paul II, but the cardinals voted instead for the more conservative Cardinal Ratzinger, now Pope Benedict XVI.

Although the mainstream churches are still viable, there is a growing phenomenon today of the practice of religion becoming increasingly personalised, diverse and eclectic. As Anglican priest and academic, Gary Bouma, states in his article 'From Hegemony to Pluralism', 'active participation in formally organised religion, churches, synagogues, mosques

---

[159] J. Griffith, *Seeking Sophia*, p. 23.

and temples is a feature of the minority, the remnant, and the diaspora'.[160] He comments:

> Diversity is now so pervasive that religious groups are internally diverse and many do not provide embracing, overarching, totalising meaning for their adherents. Their meanings have become one set among others, which is made even more complex by the rise of profound levels of internal diversity within religious groups. Those who insist that religious groups speak with a single voice are harking back to the former order.[161]

For women the spiritual quest is for a religion or form of Christianity in which they can sense that they have full personhood, that equality of the sexes is not only taken for granted but is embedded in church ethics and ecclesiology.

Christian women scholars are researching assiduously to bring fresh insights to both scripture and theology. An example of this can be found in Professor Elaine Wainwright's two works *Towards a Feminist Critical Reading of the Gospel According to Matthew* and *Shall we Look for Another? A Feminist Reading of the Matthean Jesus.*[162] But,

---

[160] Gary D. Bouma, 'From Hegemony to Pluralism: Managing Religious Diversity in Modernity and Post-Modernity', *Australian Religious Studies Review*, Vol. 12, No. 2, Spring 1999, p. 21.

[161] *Ibid.*

[162] Elaine M. Wainwright, *Towards a Feminist Critical Reading of the Gospel According to Matthew*, De Gruyter, Berlin, 1991 and Elaine M. Wainwright, *Shall we Look for Another?: A Feminist Reading of the Matthean Jesus*, Cross Books, Maryknoll, New York, 1998.

as Gillian Paterson admits, although the women's movement has friends among male pastors and theologians, 'the overall response of the male-stream academic establishment is either to try to co-opt (and therefore control) feminist theology, or else to discredit it.'[163]

It is crucial today to educate grassroots Christians, women in particular, that the Christian God is a God who honours women's experience, even if the male Church is sending out contradictory signals.[164] As Irja Askola of Finland admits: 'Feminist theology changed my life and gave language to my feelings', continuing,

> Traditional theology confirms dualism. Feminist theology brings together heart and mind. It is no longer either/or. What feminist theology has to offer to the world is the opportunity to be fully alive.[165]

The 21st century has opened with startling revelations of sexual abuse and paedophilia in mainstream churches, especially in Roman Catholicism. Benedictine sister and academic, Joan Chittister, in her paper 'The Faith will Survive', questions what it is in the clerical culture itself which leads to this problem arising:

> There are three dimensions of ecclesiastical medievalism that are still part and parcel of the church today. These were once effective and

---
[163] Gillian Paterson, *Still Flowing*, p. 111.
[164] *Ibid*.
[165] Cited in *Ibid*.

perhaps even necessary to the security of the state, but they're now long gone in the politics and processes of the rest of the world. The culture of silence, the culture of exclusion, and the culture of domination, all elements of a clerical world, lead to the very fiasco that brings good people - priests, bishops, and cardinals among them - to make choices geared more to saving the system than to saving the people ... The church forgets at its peril that even monarchies are these days subject to both public scrutiny and legal accountability.[166]

Chittister points out that the culture of silence requires that 'the business and decisions, agendas and processes, struggles and conflicts of a closed system be hidden entirely from public view'. Silence hides problems in order to deny them. The closed system buys silence from others so that the rest of the society can never know that they are also in danger. Chittister believes that people will begin to make a distinction between the faith they hold and the authorities they follow. She believes that it will be the authorities, not the faith, who will stand to lose.

In his recently published book, *A Long Way from Rome*, Catholic journalist, Chris McGillion, argues that 'the sexual abuse crisis within the church... has undermined the moral credibility of the church, undermined the authority of the church leaders and priests in many ways'. McGillion believes

---

[166] Joan Chittister, 'The Faith will Survive', *Sojourners' Magazine*, July-August, 2002, Vol. 32, No. 4, pp. 20-21.

that this has led to a dramatic decline in church attendance, which has been much more serious than over the same period in any other church.[167] In particular, numbers of youthful people have left the church, though the lyrics of pop music indicate that there is a spiritual thirst in the younger generations.

It is very difficult for clergy to criticise their bishops, even when they recognise, through working at the grassroots level, that the hierarchy's conservative statements are turning the younger generations away from the church. Bishops have control over career paths and promotion, and they are known to favour those who toe the conservative line. Dissent has traditionally been the sphere of the prophets and the reformists.

So, the price Christians pay when they cry out for reform is very high, probably one of the reasons why disillusioned Christians are leaving the mainstream and establishing more user-friendly, and to their way of thinking, more ethical, worshipping communities. Being marginalised and oppressed is at the heart of the dynamic which has driven and still drives the Christian women's reform movements. Gender injustices built into ecclesial structures provide the incentive for women to seek change. Resistance is often empowering, bringing a new self-esteem to churchwomen, enabling them to stand up to the flak which they inevitably receive from authority figures.

It is on the level of consciousness about the need for renewal that change will occur. Traditional ways of being

---

[167] C. McGillion, *A Long Way from Rome: Why the Australian Catholic Church is in Crisis*, Allen and Unwin, Sydney, 2003.

Christian act to dull consciousness; they encourage passive acceptance. Women as a group, sharing an awareness of marginalisation and speaking out against ecclesial injustice, provide Christian churches with an alternative perspective, directing them towards a different construction of Christianity.

Churchwomen will have to make clear that they are not mounting resistance against the true God, nor denying the leadership of Jesus Christ. They are correcting the humanly created male bias, which has plagued Christianity for almost two thousand years. Theologians, biblical scholars, and liturgists will need to work out, in conjunction with churchwomen, how to eradicate any impression that the divine can only be imaged in masculine categories. Love and respect for all people must be the prevailing ethos for the Third Millennium.

www.ingramcontent.com/pod-product-compliance
Lightning Source LLC
Chambersburg PA
CBHW010245010526
44107CB00063B/2691